Addison

To Dave,

On our 10th Wedding Anniversary
With much love

from Carol
x x x x x

D1806556

# The
# Cheshire
# Lines
# Committee

## Then and Now

# The Cheshire Lines Committee

## Then and Now

*Nigel Dyckhoff*

LONDON

IAN ALLAN LTD

First published 1984

ISBN 0 7110 1410 8

© Ian Allan Ltd 1984

Published by Ian Allan Ltd, Shepperton, Surrey;
and printed by Ian Allan Printing Ltd at their
works at Coombelands in Runnymede, England.

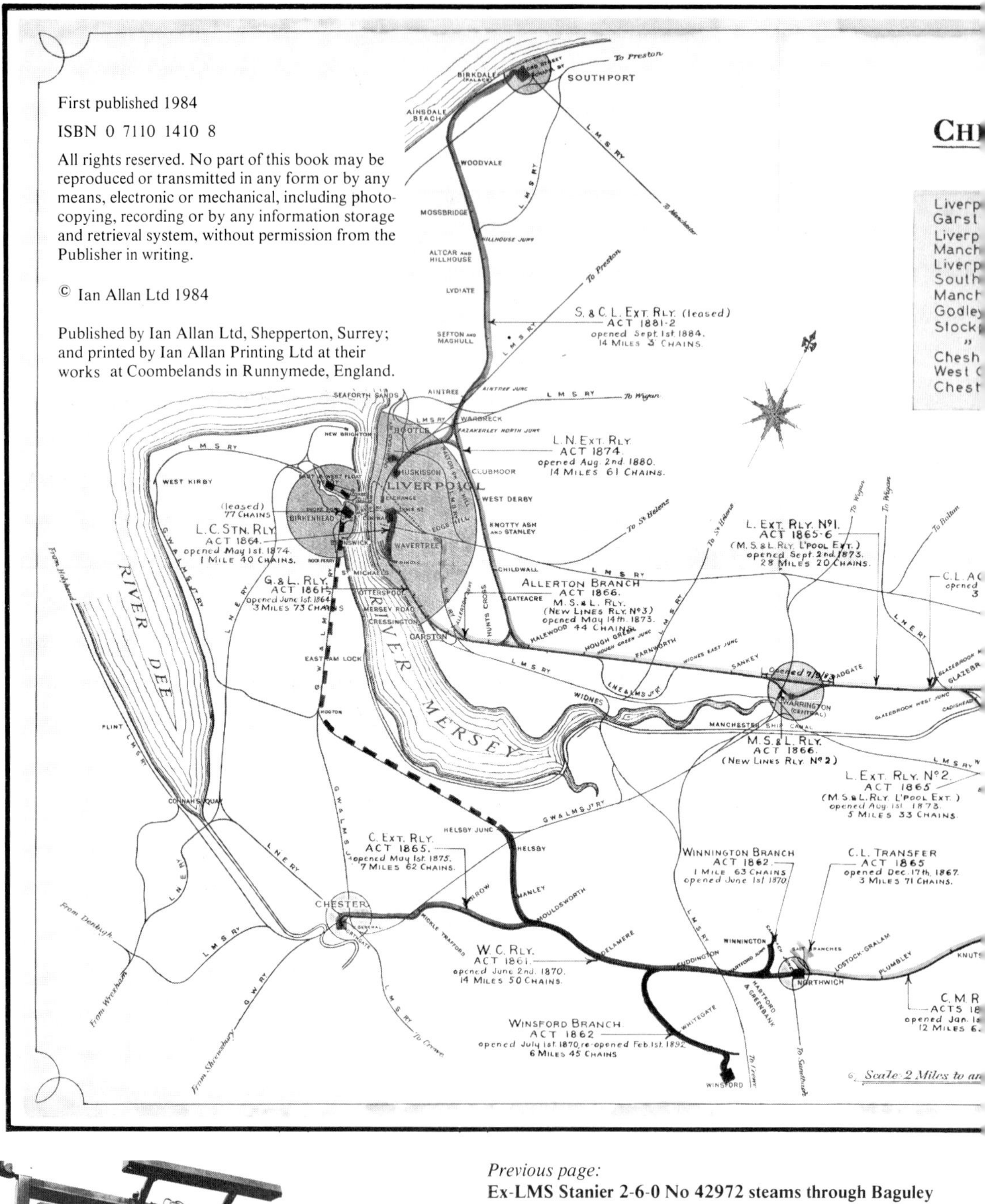

*Previous page:*
**Ex-LMS Stanier 2-6-0 No 42972 steams through Baguley
station with an empty wagon train 31 March 1965.**
*N. F. W. Dyckhoff*

*Above:*
**Map prepared by the CLC Engineers' Office in 1935.
Dates shown may be at variance with other sources. In the
text all quoted dates are taken from 'Chronology of the
Railways of Lancashire and Cheshire' compiled by M. D.
Greville. All other maps used in the book also belonged to
the CLC and show (shaded) land owned, purchased and
sold.**

# LINES RAILWAY.

## — REFERENCE. —

| | |
|---|---|
| on Rlys. Nos. 1 & 2. shewn thus | ▭ |
| rpool Rly. | ,, ,, |
| Station Rly. | ,, ,, |
| ,, ,, | ,, ,, |
| Extension Rly. | ,, ,, |
| .L. ,, ,, | ,, ,, |
| District ,, | ,, ,, |
| ley Rly. | ,, ,, |
| Woodley Rly. | ,, ,, |
| & Altrincham Jc.Rly. | ,, ,, |
| d Rly. | ,, ,, |
| tly. | ,, ,, |
| on Rly. | ,, ,, |

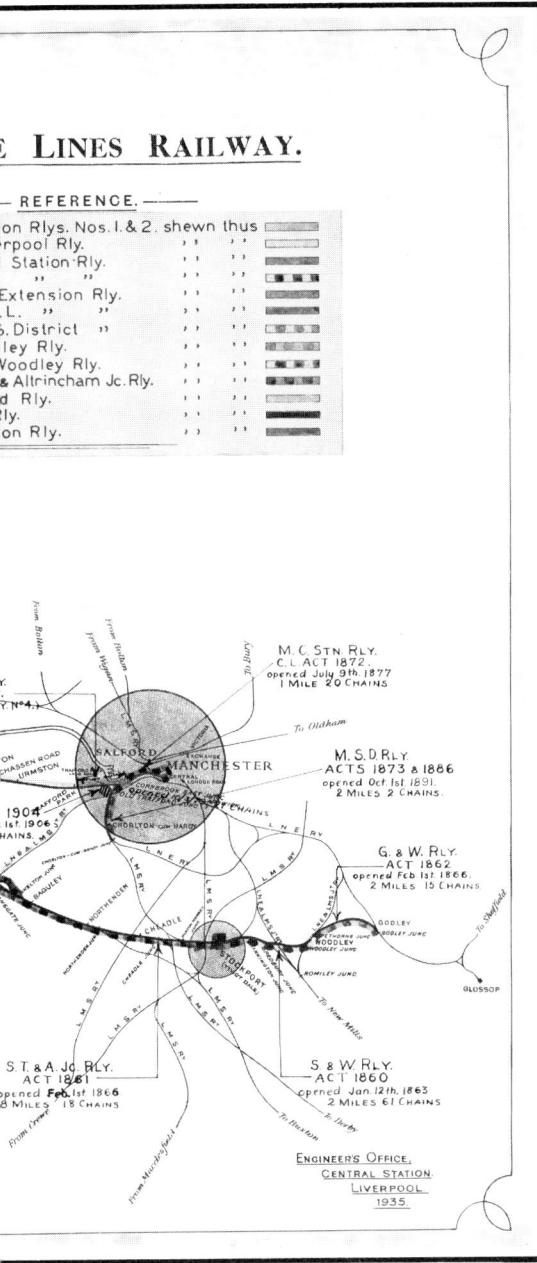

M. C. STN. RLY.
C.L. ACT 1872.
opened July 9th 1877
1 MILE 20 CHAINS

M.S.D RLY.
ACTS 1873 & 1886
opened Oct 1st 1891.
2 MILES 2 CHAINS

G. & W. RLY.
ACT 1862
opened Feb 1st 1866.
2 MILES 15 CHAINS

S.T. & Jc. RLY.
ACT 1851
opened Feb 1st 1866.
8 MILES 18 CHAINS

S. & W. RLY.
ACT 1860
opened Jan. 12th 1863
2 MILES 61 CHAINS

ENGINEER'S OFFICE,
CENTRAL STATION.
LIVERPOOL
1935.

---

**LIST OF CHESHIRE LINES STATIONS, SHEWING THE ACCOMMODATION PROVIDED AT EACH FOR DEALING WITH TRAFFIC.**

| STATIONS. | STATION ACCOMMODATION. | | | | MAXIMUM CRANE POWER. | |
|---|---|---|---|---|---|---|
| | | | | | TONS | CWT. |
| Aintree | † G | P | — | — | 5 | 0 |
| Altcar & Hillhouse | § G | P | F | L | 5 | 0 |
| Ashley | — G | P | — | L | 5 | 0 |
| Baguley | § G | P | F | L | 5 | 0 |
| Barrow for Tarvin | § G | P | F | L | 5 | T0 |
| Birkdale | § G | P | — | L | 5 | 0 |
| Birkenhead (Shore Road) | — G | — | F | L | 40 | 0 |
| Brunswick, L'pool | § G | — | F | L | 40 | 0 |
| Cadishead | — G | P | — | — | — | |
| Cheadle | § G | P | F | L | 5 | 0 |
| Chester (N'gate) | § G | P | F | L | 10 | 0 |
| Childwall | — G | P | — | — | — | |
| Chorlton-cum-Hardy | § G | P | F | L | 5 | 0 |
| Cornbrook (see Manchester) | — | — | — | — | — | |
| Cressington and Grassendale | — G | P | — | — | — | |
| Cuddington | § G | P | F | L | 5 | 0 |
| Delamere | § G | P | F | L | 5 | 0 |
| Farnworth | — G | P | F | L | 5 | 0 |
| Flixton | § G | P | F | L | 5 | 0 |
| Garston (Pas'ger) | § — | P | F | L | — | |
| Garston (Goods) | — G | — | — | — | 5 | 0 |
| Gateacre | § G | P | F | L | 5 | T0 |
| Glazebrook | § G | P | F | L | 5 | 0 |
| Godley | — G | P | — | — | — | |
| Hale | § G | P | F | L | 5 | 0 |
| Halewood | — G | P | — | — | — | |
| Hartford and Greenbank | † G | P | — | L | 5 | 0 |
| Helsby and Alvanley | § G | * | F | L | 5 | 0 |
| Hough Green | § G | P | F | L | 5 | 0 |
| Hunt's Cross | — G | P | — | — | — | |
| Huskisson, L'pool | § G | P | F | L | 36 | 0 |
| Irlam | § G | P | F | L | 5 | 0 |
| Knotty Ash and Stanley | § G | P | F | L | 5 | 0 |
| Knutsford | § G | P | F | L | 5 | 0 |
| Liverpool (C.) | § — | P | F | — | 1 | 0 |

| STATIONS. | STATION ACCOMMODATION. | | | | MAXIMUM CRANE POWER. | |
|---|---|---|---|---|---|---|
| | | | | | TONS | CWT. |
| Lostock Gralam | † G | P | — | L | 5 | 0 |
| Lydiate | § G | P | F | L | 5 | 0 |
| Manchester (C.) | § — | P | — | — | — | |
| Manchester (G.) | — G | — | F | — | 22 | 0 |
| Do. Cornbrook | — G | — | F | L | 5 | 0 |
| Manley | — G | — | — | — | — | |
| Mersey Road and Aigburth | — G | P | — | — | — | |
| Mickle Trafford | — G | P | — | L | 5 | T0 |
| Mobberley | § G | P | F | L | 5 | 0 |
| Mossbridge | — G | P | — | — | — | |
| Mouldsworth | § G | P | F | L | 5 | 0 |
| Northenden | — § G | P | — | L | 5 | 0 |
| Northwich | § G | P | F | L | 5 | 0 |
| Otterspool | — G | P | — | — | — | |
| Padgate | † G | P | — | L | 5 | 0 |
| Partington | § G | P | F | L | 5 | 0 |
| Plumbley | — G | P | — | L | 5 | 0 |
| Portwood | — G | — | — | — | — | |
| Sankey | § G | P | F | L | 5 | 0 |
| Seaside | — G | P | — | — | — | |
| Sefton & Maghull | — G | P | F | L | 5 | 0 |
| Southport | § G | P | F | L | 10 | 0 |
| St. James's | — G | P | — | — | — | |
| St. Michael's | — G | P | — | — | — | |
| Stockport (G'ds) | — G | — | F | L | 10 | 0 |
| Stockport (Tiviot Dale) | § — | P | — | — | — | |
| Trafford Park | — G | P | — | — | — | |
| Urmston | § G | P | F | L | 5 | 0 |
| Walton-on-the-Hill | — G | P | — | — | 5 | 0 |
| Warrington | § G | P | F | L | 10 | 0 |
| Wavertree and Edge Hill, L'pool | — G | — | F | L | 10 | 0 |
| West Derby | § G | P | F | L | 5 | 0 |
| West Timperley | — G | P | — | — | — | |
| Whitegate | — G | P | — | — | 5 | T0 |
| Winnington | — G | * | — | — | — | |
| Winsford & Over | § G | P | F | L | 5 | 0 |
| Woodvale | § G | P | F | L | 5 | 0 |

* Parcels only.
† Horses only.    § Horses and Carriages.    **G**—Goods Station.

**F**—Provided with Accommodation for Loading and Unloading Furniture Vans, Portable Engines, and Machines on Wheels.

**P**—Passenger Station.    **L**—Live Stock.    **T**—Travelling Crane by arrangement.

---

# Contents

*Left:*
**Inn sign from the public house opposite Hale station, 21 July 1983.** *N. F. W. Dyckhoff*

*Above right:*
**A page from the CLC Appendix to the working Timetable: 3 March 1907 and until further notice.**

# Preface

Considering its importance, both nationally (it has strong claims to be the premier joint line), and locally (it linked some of the most thriving centres in Lancashire and Cheshire) perhaps it is surprising how little has been published concerning the Cheshire Lines Committee. A short, but definitive history, written by an employee with access to company records was issued on the demise of the Committee at nationalisation. It is still in print and has been revised and extended. Also the histories of the owning companies; the Great Central, Great Northern and Midland Railways, cover the CLC appropriately. But there have been few photographic treatments and this volume sets out to remedy this omission.

The reason for this lack of photographic coverage seems clear: because the CLC never owned its own locomotives — always using those of its owners — photographers did not visit the line. They could see and photograph MS&LR/GCR, GNR, MR and later LMS and LNER locomotives on their home ground. By the time railway photographers were becoming interested in more than just the train, the CLC had lost its independence and was, however gradually, losing its identity in the London Midland Region of British Railways. The search for suitable photographs has therefore been the most challenging task in the preparation of this book. Sincere thanks are due to the photographers and collectors credited under the published pictures, who have allowed them to reach a wider audience.

My interest in the CLC stems from boyhood. Part of the line was an easy bicycle ride from home, so it was natural that when I picked up a camera I should use it there. As the first of my railway photographs to be published was taken on the CLC, the start of a love affair is easy to understand. An observant reader will identify my favourite haunts. One of the pleasures of producing this volume has been to see other photographers' views of the same places; another to go back and photograph present day operations at those locations that remain.

In selecting the photographs, preference has been given to those previously unpublished and only those taken on tracks owned by or leased to the CLC have been included. I have tried to give an impression of the railway over its independent life and to the present day, as a changing but significant part of the locality it serves. This has meant, wherever possible, choosing shots that 'stand back' and show the railway in its environment. At the same time an effort has been made to include as many as possible of the various classes of locomotive that have worked on the line, the different styles of station and signalbox, signalling and lineside furniture, the ephemera and of course the staff who served the

CLC. Even 35 years later, pride in the Cheshire Lines is still real for those who were its employees, as is the genuine affection felt for the railway by those who used it.

No history, even one primarily in pictures, can be complete without an introduction. This one has been written to stimulate interest and is my view of the CLC. I hope the reader will be encouraged to learn more about this attractive railway and if possible, to visit and enjoy what is left.

It is too easily forgotten that a work like this one can only be produced with the unstinting help of fellow enthusiasts and of those individuals, often without a personal interest in railways, who are nevertheless willing to facilitate an author's search. All are listed below and this book is dedicated to them. Should an oversight have caused the omission of the names of one or two people who know that they helped, I apologise and assure them that their assistance is very much appreciated.

**Acknowledgements**

Two people must be singled out for special mention: Bob Miller, CLC Steward of the Historical Model Railway Society and David Clough, both of whom have given me considerable encouragement and information. Others who have played a part are: Matt Aldred; Sir Peter Allen; Philip Atkins; R. T. Bateman; Arnold Battson; Michael Bentley; Gordon Biddle; Alan Bolton; Michael Brackett; John Brewer; D. J. W. Brough; L. Brown; Roy Burrows; David J. Chinery; Gordon Coltas; Ivor Cowdy; C. N. Crofts; Andrew Cross; Trefor David; David Deakin; George Dow; Andrew and Martin Dyckhoff; Jim Ferguson; Michael Gillings; Larry Goddard; Maryann Gomez; C. Tony Goode; R. S. Greenwood; Mrs Jill Groves; R. H. N. Hardy; Mrs Ann Harris; E. Harrison; J. Hatch; Ron Herbert; Peter Holmes; G. O. Holt; Mike Howarth; Robert Humm; James Hunt; D. Ibbotson; David Jackson; Basil Jeuda; Emma Jones; A. Leigh; Brian W. Leslie; Harold Livesey; J. Lomas; K. McDougall; J. S. McGahey; G. Moorcroft; N. R. Nutter; Eric Oldham; John Owen; R. H. S. Owen; Miss S. Owen; Sir Peter Parker MVO; Hubert Parrish; Stephen Patrick; Caroline Phelps; Bob Pue; John Quick; Hugh D. Ramsey; David I. Rapson; D. K. Redford CBE DL; R. C. Riley; R. E. Rose; Peter Semmens; F. W. Shuttleworth; Capt Bill Smith; Brian Stevenson; Neville Stead; Laura Stirling-Aird; M. S. Stokes; Neville R. Thompson; G. Turnbull; P. Tuson; Michael White; Professor Pat White; Denis Wilcox; F. Williams.

*Nigel F. W. Dyckhoff*
*Llanddewi Velfrey, Narberth*

# Introduction

Man's ambition was never so clearly seen as a driving force as when the railways of Britain were built. It is to this that the Cheshire Lines Committee owes its existence: the man, Edward (later Sir Edward) Watkin, his railway, the Manchester, Sheffield & Lincolnshire and their first ally the Great Northern Railway. Both companies sought to reach the district west and southwest of Manchester then dominated by the London & North Western Railway. When the Midland Railway joined them as an equal partner in 1866 and a year later the Cheshire Lines Committee achieved independent management, it became the company it was to remain until nationalisation in 1948.

## The Early Years

What was arguably Britain's most successful joint line had its beginnings in a railway just over two and a half miles long. This was the Stockport and Woodley Junction Railway (S&WJR) promoted locally in 1860 to link the Manchester, Sheffield & Lincolnshire Railway (MS&LR) line from Manchester to Marple with a station in the Cheshire market town of Stockport. Watkin was a noted railwayman. At various times on the Boards of the Great Western and Great Eastern Railways and President of the Grand Trunk of Canada he was not only Chairman of the MS&LR but also of the South Eastern, Metropolitan and East London Railways, with which empire he pursued his dream of a Channel Tunnel. He almost certainly exerted behind the scenes influence on the formation of the S&WJR as he did on the Cheshire Midland Railway (CMR), another local line incorporated in the same year. This was to leave the Manchester South Junction & Altrincham Railway (MSJ&AR) at its terminus in Altrincham and run to Northwich $12\frac{1}{4}$ miles distant. The MS&LR was authorised to subscribe to its capital. The CMR opened in two stages, from Altrincham to Knutsford on 12 May 1862 and from Knutsford to Northwich on 1 January 1863. It was linked with the S&WJR by the Stockport, Timperley & Altrincham Junction Railway (SJ&AJR), nine miles long and separately incorporated in 1861, which opened on 1 February 1866. At the same time a branch from Woodley to Godley, which had been sanctioned in 1862, was opened.

In 1861 the West Cheshire Railway Act authorised the construction of a line from Northwich to Helsby (WCR) where it formed a junction with the Birkenhead Joint Line (Great Western and London & North Western). The following year further powers were obtained to construct the Winsford and Winnington branches. Northwich to Helsby opened for passengers on 22 June 1870 and Cuddington to Winsford and Over on 1 July 1870, a month after the Winnington branch had opened to goods traffic only.

All the undertakings described so far (apart from a short portion of line near Stockport) were in Cheshire so it was entirely appropriate that when they were put together they should be called the 'Cheshire Lines'. The first step towards joining them up was through the Great Northern and Manchester, Sheffield & Lincolnshire Joint Committee, which represented the common interests of the GNR and MS&LR. By means of the Great Northern (Cheshire Lines) Act of 1863 the GNR obtained powers to subscribe to, and pay interest on the capital of, the four railway companies; S&WJR, CMR, ST&AJR and WCR. The Midland Railway (MR) which gained its access to Manchester over the MS&LR was also concerned to draw traffic from West Lancashire and Cheshire and sought admission to the partnership. The four lines were vested jointly in the three parent companies by an Act of 5 July 1865 and the Cheshire Lines Committee (CLC) had begun.

The MR took up membership in 1866 and in 1867 the CLC became an independent entity. Uniquely for this country it did not have the word 'Railway' in its title nor did it have shareholders, being owned equally by the MS&LR, GNR and MR. Its management was controlled by a committee of nine members, three from each company. The first manager of the CLC was William English, who in 1863 had become the first officer of the joint line when he was appointed manager of the Garston and Liverpool Railway (G&LR) on its opening on 1 June 1864. It had been swept into the CLC by the above mentioned Cheshire Lines Transfer Act of 1865.

By 1866 it was possible to travel from Godley on the MS&LR main line, via Woodley and through Stockport Tiviot Dale (which then became the main station supplanting Portwood), on through Cheadle and Northenden to Deansgate Junction with the MSJ&AR and Broadheath Junction with the Warrington & Stockport Railway (W&SR). The W&SR had ended at Timperley and together with the St Helens Railway became part of the LNWR in 1864. Running powers over these lines gave the CLC access to its own rails at Garston and thus its entry to Liverpool. Running powers over the MSJ&AR as far as Altrincham linked the CLC with its own metals in a similar way to give it access to Northwich and Helsby Junction.

It had early been realised that Brunswick was too far out of town to be a satisfactory Liverpool terminal. Horse buses were used to meet the trains and carry passengers to the CLC offices in James Street. The bus wheels, to standard gauge, ran for part of the journey on dockside lines for smoothness of passage. In July 1864 the Liverpool Central Station Railway was incorporated to extend from Brunswick to a station in Ranelagh Street; Liverpool Central. This required a tunnel through rock and an intermediate station at St James (closed 1916). It took 10 years to build. Chester was reached by means of the Chester & West Cheshire Junction Railway which was incorporated in July 1865 and opened in November 1874. Like the extension to Liverpool Central, completion was delayed by a shortage of funds. It ran from a junction at Mouldsworth on the WCR to Chester, Northgate. A connection with the LNWR/GWR joint line at Mickle Trafford was put in but never used.

The major step in the final shape of the CLC was the construction of its own main line between Manchester and Liverpool. On the completion of the link via the LNWR line between Broadheath Junction and Garston, services had been run between Manchester Oxford Road, (using the MSJ&AR) and Liverpool Brunswick. But despite obtaining similar running powers over equally lengthy stretches of the then two partners' own metals — to Sheffield via the MS&LR and Grimsby and New Holland via the GNR — the LNWR was as obstructive as possible to the new service. It was aided in this by the fact that the route had 95 level crossings over its length and some severe speed restrictions at the Manchester end.

Watkin, whose expansionist outlook could rarely be contained, determined to escape from what he called the 'running powers' line'. On behalf of the MS&LR he deposited a Bill for a line from Old Trafford on the MSJ&AR (later amended to Cornbook) to a junction with the G&LR near Cressington; and from Glazebrook on this new line to the ST&AJR at Skelton Junction. He was confident that he would soon have the support of the Midland as well as the Great Northern and this proved to be the case. Both these railways were concerned about a proposed amalgamation between the Lancashire & Yorkshire Railway (L&YR) and the Great Eastern Railway (GER) and thus had special reasons for working to strengthen themselves in Lancashire. So they supported the MS&LR, even if for political rather than straight commercial reasons, against determined opposition from the LNWR and L&YR.

The new line was sanctioned in July 1865 despite this opposition and that of local landowners and traders on the Sankey Canal. It seems that the House of Commons Committee was most convinced by the argument that existing facilities were insufficient to meet the needs of two important communities and by the slow journey time of existing trains (few did the distance between Manchester and Liverpool in less than an hour). This was a notable defeat for the LNWR and led to strained relations for many years.

Work began quickly and Watkin's judgement on the new lines' value was vindicated when, in 1866, it was vested in the CLC — so making the GNR and MR each responsible for one third of the costs of construction. Delays occurred, caused first by an economic recession and then by shortages of labour and bad weather. The section from Skelton Junction to Cressington Junction opened on 1 March 1873 while passenger services on the new direct line from Manchester started on 2 September 1873. Trains travelled via the loop at Warrington, as due to public pressure for a station nearer the town centre, this was constructed first. The so-called 'straight line' used by trains to avoid Warrington, although it had been sanctioned before the loop line, was not opened until 10 years later.

The MR had gained its first access to Manchester by its Act of 1862 which secured it entry to Manchester London Road station over the MS&LR from New Mills. Through passenger services from London began on 1 February 1867, initially starting at King's Cross, but on 1 October 1868 the MR opened their extension to London St Pancras. From the opening of the new CLC line to Liverpool the Midland had access to that city also, but in a most unsatisfactory way. Because trains could not be divided at Woodley (the Midlands entry point to the CLC), London to Liverpool carriages had to run into Manchester London Road and back out again. This problem had been foreseen and powers obtained in 1866 to build a line from Ashburys to Brinnington Junction on the S&WJR and a branch to Romiley on the Marple line. The promoter was the MS&LR with the understanding that the Midland would become joint owners. A modification was made in 1869, the 'Marple Curve', which gave the Midland direct access to the CLC from the south. It was so named because when services over it began in 1875 the interchange point became Marple station — the curve was actually between Romiley Junction and Bredbury Junction.

One of the results of the construction of the new CLC main line from Manchester to Liverpool and the consequent sorry relations with the LNWR was a plan to build a new and much more central station in Manchester. Regrettably for future transport needs, this came to nothing. Nevertheless the facilities at Manchester Oxford Road were soon inadequate for the volume of traffic using them and in 1872, powers were obtained by the CLC for a new independent terminus to be named Manchester Central. This was opened on 9 July 1877, but was only intended to be temporary, as in 1875 Parliamentary approval had been granted for a more permanent station. This became the present Manchester Central opened on 1 July 1880.

With the increasing traffic coming from the MR now that it had a route to Manchester (and over the CLC on to Liverpool) together with a general growth of MS&LR traffic as the recession that had followed boom in the mid-1860s disappeared, chronic congestion developed at Manchester London Road station and its approaches. In 1875 the MS&LR

gave the MR three years notice to quit and so obliged them to find another station in Manchester. This same year the CLC had obtained powers to build the new Manchester Central station, leaving the temporary one to become a CLC goods depot. With the MR a partner in the CLC it was natural that the railway should try to gain access to the new Central station.

In 1873 the Manchester South District Railway (MSDR) had been incorporated to build a line from Manchester to Alderley. Nothing had been done by 1875 when the MR proposed that the portion north of Stockport should become part of the CLC and so give it entry to Manchester Central. The GNR would not agree and more strangely nor would Watkin, who was at first overruled by his colleagues. In 1877 he got his way and the MSDR was vested solely in the MR. Remodelled to meet to the MR's needs, the line opened on 1 January 1880 from Heaton Mersey Junction to Throstle Nest Junction on the CLC near Cornbrook. The MR now had its access and after the opening of the new Manchester Central station withdrew its trains from London Road on 1 August 1880. Henceforth all MR services used Central station. Ironically, in 1891, the section from Throstle Nest Junction to Chorlton Junction (the point where a new MS&LR line from Fairfield on the London Road to Guide Bridge line entered) was transferred to the ownership of the CLC.

The final element in the MR approach to Manchester was the construction of its direct line to bypass Marple and Stockport Tiviot Dale, both stations suffering considerable congestion by the late 1890s. The first part of the 'new line' was opened in 1901 from Heaton Mersey to Cheadle Heath (built to serve outer Stockport) and the remainder in 1902.

When the new Liverpool Central station opened on 2 March 1874 the original station at Brunswick became a goods depot. It gave access to Brunswick Dock, but only at the southern end of a system which stretched six miles northwards and where both the LNWR and L&YR enjoyed better facilities. To compete for a larger share of traffic the CLC puchased 23 acres of land in the Huskisson area and was then faced with the problem of reaching the site. Rejecting the prohibitively expensive alternative of a low level line through Liverpool from Central station, the CLC chose to construct a previously considered rail connection to the north of Liverpool. Officially known as the North Liverpool Line, it was authorised in July 1874 and included a line from junctions at Hunts Cross and Halewood to a junction with the L&YR between Aintree and Maghull, as well as a line from Fazakerley to Walton-on-the-Hill. It opened on 1 December 1879 and the extension to Huskisson followed on 1 July 1880. A number of intermediate stations were provided.

With its line to Aintree built, the CLC was now only 14 miles from Southport, already well known as

a seaside resort. Following deputations from the town residents the CLC agreed to sponsor a separate company to be known as the Southport & Cheshire Lines Extension Railway (S&CLER). Incorporated by Acts in August 1881 and August 1882, it was constructed speedily, and opened to its terminus in Lord Street, Southport, on 1 September 1884. The railway was never part of the CLC but agreement was reached to work it 'in perpetuity'. It was therefore considered an integral part of the network, unlike later extensions to St Helens, Wigan and Widnes, which remained in entirely separate ownership although closely linked for operating purposes.

Had Watkin had his way, a connection with the Mersey Railway in Liverpool might have led to the CLC having control of it and so gaining direct access to Birkenhead and the goods depots. As it was, these could only be reached via Helsby and the Birkenhead Joint Line. But Watkin's ambition over-reached itself and all that remained of his plan was a low level station built by the Mersey Railway beneath the CLC at Central station and opened on 11 January 1892. Later efforts to link with the Liverpool Overhead Railway were equally unsuccessful.

Now began many years of prosperity for the CLC and useful service to the area it covered. It is hard for us now to imagine how fierce the competition was between the different railway companies and how determinedly they fought for territorial advantage that would bring them traffic. Today's best analogy is probably found in supermarket chains who compete locally and nationally; who take each other over and who develop from enlarged corner shops to super stores. For the LNWR, read Marks and Spencer; for GNR, read Sainsbury; for MR, read Tesco and for MS&LR, read Asda. Fanciful perhaps, but a point is made and the completed CLC in the first year of the 20th century was well placed to give its three owners a worthwhile share of some profitable traffic.

Foremost for passenger business were the trains between Liverpool and Manchester. Known throughout Lancashire and Cheshire as the 'Punctual Service', the timetable came into operation on the opening of the temporary Central station in Manchester. It was very much better than services provided by the CLC's competitors, the LNWR and L&YR, by their direct routes. Express trains ran hourly in each direction, at half past the hour from each terminus, and with a journey time (including a stop a Warrington) of 45 minutes. After the Warrington straight line was opened in 1883, some non-stop trains did the journey in 40 minutes. With very little alteration, the same service was provided up to the beginning of World War 2. On its introduction, fares were reduced and cheap fare facilities provided for the first time. So successful was this operation that Watkin tried hard to persuade his partners to consent to a half hourly service, but to no avail.

An intensive service of stopping trains also ran and these led to a considerable growth in commuter traffic to Manchester, with the development of new suburbs around Urmston, Flixton and Irlam. The same effect was seen on the line to Chester, particularly at Peel Causeway (later renamed Hale) and on the Manchester South District line at Chorlton-cum-Hardy. Possibly this well known verse dates from that time:

*They sleep in Hale and Sale by night,*
*In Manchester by day,*
*They travel by the CLC*
*And MSJ&A.*

In the same way, at the Liverpool end of the line thousands of 'contractors', as season ticket-holders were then called, travelled to Central station daily from Gateacre, West Derby, Garston, Cressington, Mersey Road and St Michaels.

Through Midland services to Manchester came into Central station via Chorlton Junction; the services to Liverpool and Southport came on to CLC metals at Bredbury Junction. In these days of HSTs and permanently coupled stock the concept of a through carriage, which passengers joined at their departure station and which was then put on and taken off other trains on other lines until it reached its ultimate destination, has been forgotten. But by this means, in the heyday of the Midland Pullman services, passengers were able to reach both Liverpool and Southport, as they had years earlier reached Manchester via Marple, in luxurious comfort. No standing around on draughty platforms waiting for a DMU connection for these fortunate travellers! There were also through carriages from the Great Northern which came via Godley Junction as did the regular connecting services from the MS&LR. A through service of trains ran from Liverpool, Southport and the rest of the CLC system to Sheffield, Nottingham, Hull, Grimsby Docks and London. In 1897 the MS&LR became the Great Central Railway (GCR) to mark the achievement of trunk line status with the building of its own independent line to London. When this opened in 1899 the CLC was linked by through services with the three London termini of its owning partners — Marylebone (GCR), King's Cross (GNR) and St Pancras (MR).

In addition to these major connections the CLC also joined with the GCR at Chester Liverpool Road giving it access to Wrexham and North Wales and at Glazebrook for Wigan and St Helens. It joined with the Sheffield and Midland Joint railway to serve Widnes. Other connections with competing railways saw varied use over the years.

Apart from regular through services other important sources of passenger traffic from outside the CLC system included sea voyagers to and from Liverpool, special race traffic to Chester, Aintree and Manchester (horsebox specials from the GER), and large numbers of holiday and excursion trains in the summer months. The Isle of Man, North Wales seaside towns and, of course, Southport (the Flower Show began in Victoria Park in 1924) were all popular. Trains bearing passengers for these destinations started both on the CLC and on its owners' lines. There were also trains run for special events of a more local kind such as steeplechases and that popular railway outing before the rise of the motor car, a day in the country.

Of the 67 stations open on the CLC in 1907, only a few lacked goods facilities. Most had a standard 5ton crane to facilitate the loading and unloading of wagons. There were also major warehouses at Liverpool (Huskisson and Brunswick), Manchester Central, Birkenhead (Shore Road), Stockport, Warrington, Northwich and Chester with a depot at Cornbrook. The GNR had its own facilities at Manchester Deansgate reached by a short branch from Cornbrook, while the MR used the CLC to reach its dockside facilities in Liverpool. When one reflects that around half of all goods traffic was, for most of the independent life of the CLC, carried in Private Owner railway wagons of 8, 10 or 12ton capacity (which had to be returned empty to their home base), then the length and number of trains, the extent of sidings and the amount of shunting necessary, need come as no surprise. The CLC, serving as it did important parts of the industrial North, had a full share of this class of traffic.

Important stretches of line, as far as goods traffic was concerned, were Altrincham-Mouldsworth, Northenden Junction-Skelton Junction and Liverpool-Manchester. The first became a major trunk route for cross-country freight traffic with John Summers steel works on the River Dee near Chester and the oil refinery at Stanlow. Northwich grew first as a centre for salt and then developed further as Brummer Mond expanded into ICI. This firm produced chemicals to be transported out and drew coal and stone traffic in. Most of the latter came via Northenden Junction-Skelton Junction which served as the Manchester Goods Avoiding line, and was probably one of the busiest sections of double-track railway in the country. In 1947, for example, it carried an average of $5\frac{1}{2}$ freight trains per hour in each direction. Through this section also passed the traffic to and from Warrington and Liverpool together with output from the Lancashire coalfields and other indigenous industries. Trains joined the Manchester-Liverpool line at Glazebrook East Junction, having used the CLC line that crossed the Manchester Ship Canal (MSC) at Cadishead. The Manchester-Liverpool line itself carried a great deal of goods traffic. Trafford Park at its eastern end was Britain's first and largest trading estate which at its peak provided jobs for some 50,000 workers. Other important businesses were steel at Irlam, soap and other products at CWS factories nearby and the MSC dock system. Further west came Warrington, Widnes with chemical and other factories, and then the whole Liverpool dock system. It was thus only to be expected that on the CLC revenues from goods handsomely exceeded those from passengers.

The two world wars brought extra traffic and considerable change and disruption. In World War 1 the CLC, in common with the other railway companies, became a controlled undertaking, subject to the direction of the Railway Executive Committee (REC). Various new works were carried out particularly sidings and goods accommodation. Sizeable contingents of home and colonial troops were carried, and in 1917, when the Americans joined the Allies, a large reception camp was established near to Knotty Ash and Stanley station on the North Liverpool line. The Southport and Cheshire Lines Extension section was closed to passenger traffic at the beginning of 1917 and the full service was not restored until 1 April, two years later.

World War 2 saw even more disturbance than the first. The CLC again became a controlled undertaking, this time with the LNER acting as liaison with the REC. Being so strategically placed to serve the west coast ports of Liverpool, Birkenhead and Manchester (a port by reason of the MSC), traffic density soared and in certain areas increased by as much as 200% over that in 1938. Some important new government works were constructed, of special note being the Ordnance Factory at Risley, which required a new station and sidings. The RAF depot, later USAF when the Americans again joined us in war, at Burtonwood (near Warrington) was connected by a private siding, as was the British Ethyl Corporation works at Plumley. All the extra traffic required considerable additional facilities including marshalling yards at Halewood and Walton to feed main depots at Liverpool docks; Glazebrook to serve the Lancashire Steel Corporation at Irlam and the MSC and at Trafford Park to serve the Estate and the MSC.

World War 2 saw the heavy and persistent bombing of England by enemy aircraft — something never experienced before. The CLC suffered badly especially in Liverpool, where the working of Liverpool Central station had to be suspended on various occasions. During the heavy blitz in 1941 all railway connections, apart from one link to the dock lines at Brunswick, were destroyed and out of action for some days. Huskisson goods station was rendered unusable and had to be abandoned for the duration of the war — the goods depot at Manchester Central also suffered considerable damage.

**Services after the Grouping**

Prior to 1923 Britain had around 150 independent standard gauge railways including the CLC. By means of the Railway Act of 1921 these were regrouped into four main railways — London Midland & Scottish (LMS), London & North Eastern (LNER), Great Western (GWR) and Southern (SR). Geographically the CLC would have fitted naturally into the LMS but such was the complexity of its traffic, and its importance in terms of revenue to the GNR and GCR, both of whom were to join the LNER, this proved to be impossible. Instead the CLC retained its independence, and from 1923 to 1948 was the fifth largest railway company in the UK. In 1920 its route mileage was $143\frac{1}{4}$, with nine miles laid quadruple track or more and a total length, equalled to single line and including sidings, of 435 miles. The committee of management from each of the owning partners — MS&LR (GCR after 1897), GNR and MR — now became six from the LNER and three from the LMS. Otherwise the CLC retained independent control of its operations, though from the 1930s certain of its functions such as Engineering, Estates, Solicitors, Stores and Accountancy were provided by the parent companies. Having survived World War 2 with credit, the CLC finally surrendered after 80 years of independence and on nationalisation in 1948 became part of the London Midland Region of British Railways.

Although parts of the CLC were very successful in attracting customers, others, even in the railways' prime, carried lightly loaded trains. The Southport Extension really survived on holiday and excursion traffic. The North Liverpool line faced early and severe competition from road transport. Stations between Stockport, Altrincham and Glazebrook provided few passengers and the Winsford branch became notorious when, due to poor receipts, the CLC pushed through its closure in 1931. But the real cutbacks did not start until the 1950s when British Railways faced up to commercial reality or, as others would have it, began to abdicate its responsibility for a national rail network.

First to go were individual stations such as Mickle Trafford, Otterspool and Halewood in 1951. The Southport Extension line from Aintree Central to Southport Lord Street followed in 1952. The next major closure was that of the stations on the North Liverpool line between Gateacre and Aintree which took place in 1960. Passenger services ceased between Warrington and Stockport on 30 November 1964 with the closure of all the intermediate stations between Glazebrook East Junction and Stockport Tiviot Dale. The latter station lost its service to Manchester Central via the South District line in 1967 and also closed. Manchester Central itself went in 1969, when the remaining services to Liverpool and Chester were diverted to Oxford Road station. Liverpool Central lasted a little longer, but when the Manchester trains were diverted to Lime Street station, only the service to Gateacre remained. After much argument this stopped on 17 April 1972 and Central closed together with the other stations still open on this route. Chester Northgate had closed at the end of 1969 when services from Manchester were diverted to Chester General station via a new junction at Mickle Trafford. Of the stations that remained, some suffered no more than a name change; others lost goods and/or parcels facilities before becoming unstaffed halts.

More recently there has been something of a resurgence. The line from Manchester Oxford Road to Chester continues with a regular DMU service and is fairly well patronised, particularly so in the summer. The line from Oxford Road to Hunts Cross links up with the Merseyrail system, and at Garston, Cressington, Aigburth and St Michaels the stations have been renovated and reopened. The electrified Merseyrail service runs through from Hunts Cross to Kirkby and there is now an underground station called Liverpool Central. The old CLC Central station at ground level has been demolished and replaced by a shopping precinct. Through trains continue to run between Manchester and Liverpool, though now the route is from Piccadilly (renamed from London Road after rebuilding in 1958) to Lime Street. This service, too, is operated by DMUs. Fast trains take 47 minutes from Oxford Road to Lime Street which time compares favourably with the previous CLC steam hauled service between the two Central stations and which was able to use the Warrington straight line closed 20 May 1968. A new station, Birchwood, between Padgate and Glazebrook, has been opened to serve Warrington New Town.

The importance of CLC lines for goods is declining but surviving freight traffic covers just about the full spectrum handled by BR. Most of the traditional sources survive though Liverpool Docks and Irlam steelworks no longer play any part. The siting of a Freightliner terminal at Trafford Park, adjacent to the Liverpool line, generated new business and resulted in the 25kV electrification being extended westwards from Cornbrook Junction to the terminal to render unnecessary a change of motive power at Longsight. The rest of the Liverpool line sees freight no more, as what remained has been diverted elsewhere. The line across the MSC from Glazebrook East Junction to Partington Junction was first singled and then closed from 4 July 1982. Trains to the CEGB power station at Partington and to the Shell oil refinery and chemicals plant at Carrington now run only occasionally. The Godley to Cheadle Junction section, once extremely important in bringing traffic from the Woodhead route has, like that line, closed. Now the only trains back down from Woodley to Portwood and deliver stone to the old coal drops. Trains still running through to Skelton Junction come mainly from the Hope Valley route

and include the Peak District stone trains which go on to ICI Winnington at Northwich. Other services are coal in MGR wagons to Fidlers Ferry and in mineral wagons to Garston. Manchester Corporation has built a large refuse transfer station close by Northenden Junction and Northenden goods yard is now the site of a cement terminal. Both receive trains regularly.

Traffic on the Altrincham to Mouldsworth Junction section is an extension of workings already described. Additions are the Associated Octel plant at Plumley which is still rail served and salt and chemicals from Northwich. The ex-LMS branch from Sandbach provides a source of traffic westward, as this is the route followed by most trains originating south of Crewe and bound for British Steel at Shotton and Stanlow oil refinery. As well as traffic to the refinery, the adjacent UKF fertiliser and ammonia plants at Ince generate workings to depots across the country. Trains from Seal Sands and Wilton to Runcorn finally leave CLC metals at Hartford CLC Junction and then travel the West Coast main line to Weaver Junction. Stanlow and Ince traffic uses the branch from Mouldsworth Junction to West Cheshire Junction, while services to Shotwick Sidings continue beyond Mickle Trafford (due to close 14 May 1984).

**Locomotives**

Although a complete railway in every other respect, the CLC never owned its own locomotives. In the beginning all motive power was provided by the MS&LR and this was challenged first by the Midland and then by the Great Northern. The MS&LR was reluctant to take any risk of losing the profits associated with such a provision — the CLC with its easily graded line was an ideal place to work out old engines — but eventually John Ramsbottom, former LNWR Locomotive Superintendent, was called to arbitrate. In 1882, he ruled that engines to meet purely CLC needs should continue to be provided by the MS&LR. From then on both the Midland and Great Northern provided the locomotives for their through trains while the MS&LR, as later the GLR and LNER, supplied the rest of the motive power. Sheds were provided by the CLC but their staff, like the footplate men, came from the MS&LR and its successors. Later suggestions that the CLC should change its policy and have its own locomotives, were always rebuffed. To the end the only motive power ever owned by the CLC were four Sentinel-Cammell railcars bought for local services in 1929 and scrapped towards the end of World War 2.

So any account of locomotives on the CLC begins with the MS&LR. As their designs went to be scrapped, so ex-GCR types took over and later joined by LNER locomotives, many lasted until Nationalisation. From then on ex-LMS types began to appear, soon followed by BR standard steam classes. In the late 1950s came the first diesel locomotives and DMUs. Steam finished on the CLC in 1968, but returned with the designation of Northwich as a shed to service steam-hauled railtours in the late 1970s and early 1980s. Otherwise the rails are left to diesel power alone. Because of this diversity over the years, it can be claimed that CLC metals have seen a greater variety of motive power than any comparable railway.

To start with, Sacré 2-4-0 and 4-4-0 classes worked the Liverpool to Manchester services. But the earliest class to dominate the line were the Sacré 2-2-2 locomotives, the first of which was built in 1882. By 1887 all were shedded on the CLC and they remained in charge until replaced by 'Hell Fire Jacks', the Pollitt Class 13 4-2-2s built in 1900 and his last design of locomotive. Coming to the CLC in 1904 they were in turn supplanted by Pollitt and Parker designs of 4-4-0, but stayed on secondary work until 1927. The various classes of 4-4-0 then had control of the main services. Exceptionally successful were the Pollitt-designed LNER Class D6 locomotive which lasted until after World War 2. These were replaced by Robinson 4-4-0s, LNER Class D9, drafted in from the LNER from 1933 onwards, so that by the end of 1946 the 27 survivors were all on the CLC. Held in high esteem, when the last was withdrawn in 1950 they were replaced by a surprising influx (because by then the CLC was part of the London Midland Region) of LNER Class D11/1 — the Robinson 'Directors'. Two ran regularly between Liverpool and Manchester on both fast and slow trains but most went into store at Trafford Park. By mid 1951 when a 'Director' class locomotive was seen, it was most likely to be heading a Manchester to Liverpool or Chester stopping train, the expresses having been taken over by ex-LMS Stanier Class 5 4-6-0s and Fairburn Class 4 2-6-4Ts. The last D11/1 remained on the CLC until 1958.

Passenger services from Manchester to Chester were the preserve first of Sacré 2-4-0 locomotives, then various 4-4-0s, notably the Parker designed LNER Class D7, six of which were shedded at Northwich between 1921 and 1930. These replaced by LNER Class C13 4-4-2Ts which ran the service for many years. They also powered the local trains between Manchester Central and Irlam. Most of the ex-GCR classes of 4-6-0 were seen on the CLC at one time or another, a few spent periods allocated to CLC sheds and most likely to be observed over the years were LNER Classes B7 and B9. Locomotives of other passenger classes came to the CLC on through workings, and events such as Grand National Day at Aintree brought a wide selection extending on occasions to LMS 'Jubilee' class 4-6-0s and LNER Gresley Class A3 Pacifics.

Sacré 0-6-0s were most common on early goods traffic. His Class 18 single-framed tender version

was originally designed with the CLC in mind, and the equivalent tank engine Class 18T 'Humpies' built from 1880 onwards, was allocated to the Liverpool North Extension line. Sacré designed LNER Class J12 0-6-0s spent from 1880 to 1930 in general use on heavy goods and occasional excursion work. The Parker-Pollitt 0 6 0s, LNER Class J11 'Pom-Poms' ran on the CLC from 1901 until 1953 when they were transferred away and replaced by ex-LMS motive power. As with passenger engines, at some time most standard LNER and LMS classes of goods locomotive could be seen on through workings. After nationalisation, ex-LMS types gradually took over together with BR standard locomotives in their turn. The last regular steam workings were mostly in the hands of ex-LMS Stanier Class 8F 2-8-0s and BR Standard Class 2-10-0s, very little else being left by then.

As far as diesel power is concerned, by 1960 DMUs were providing a regular interval service between Manchester and Chester. First tests of diesel locomotives on the ICI limestone trains from Tunstead to Northwich took place in June 1963. From then on, diesels became more common as the pace of steam locomotive withdrawal quickened. Nowadays, freight workings are hauled variously by Classes 25, 40 and 47 depending on the individual service. Class 37s also appear from time to time and Class 56s are seen occasionally. Crew training on Class 20 began at Northwich in 1984 and pairs of these locomotives will replace Class 25.

## Rolling Stock

The first coaches manufactured specifically for the CLC were all 4-wheeled and purchased in the mid-1860s. On the opening of the Skelton Junction to Cressington Junction section of the CLC new line, a further batch was ordered together with some carriage trucks and horseboxes. More were ordered in 1876 together with a 6-wheeled family saloon. To start with, coaches were built to MS&LR designs at Gorton, but later private builders were also used. From 1879 to 1900 12-wheeled bogie carriages were manufactured to MS&LR and GCR designs. These coaches held their own both in comfort and in decor with those of many of the larger railway companies. The CLC abolished second class in 1892 and by 1898 all coaches had been fitted with gas lighting. Filling stations were provided at Liverpool Central, Brunswick and Manchester Central and these could also be used by the parent companies for their through coaches. 4-wheeled carriages began to be replaced by new 6-wheelers from 1891 onwards and in their turn, 6-wheelers were replaced by 8-wheeled bogie stock from 1904. Wholesale scrapping of 6-wheeled carriages did not commence until about 1930.

In 1908, due to the high prices tendered by outside firms, carriages were built by the Midland and horseboxes and refrigerated meat vans by the Great Northern. Each built to its own designs of the time. The Midland used teak at extra cost rather than graining and painting. In 1911 and 1912, two large orders for bogie carriages, together with a family saloon, were completed at Doncaster with many details to standard GNR practice. The Great Central built an order in 1914 as its new works in Dukinfield and in 1920/21 refurbished numbers of 6-wheeled carriages coupling them into 12-coach sets for local services. By 1922 the CLC owned 462 passenger carriages and 91 other coaching vehicles (luggage, parcel and brake vans, carriage trucks, horse boxes etc). It also had 4,573 merchandise and mineral vehicles and 149 railway service vehicles.

The first order after grouping went to outside private builders and was for bogie carriages with electric lighting. This order was completed in 1925 and another followed immediately. In 1927 the Board approved a recommendation by the parent companies that CLC stock should henceforth be maintained at the number, including duplicates, given in the 1922 published accounts. From that time forward only renewals could take place, and in 1928 both Cravens and LNER Dukinfield works supplied carriages. In 1930 coaches were transferred from both the LMS and LNER and when the MSJ&AR was electrified in 1931, their stock of steam hauled bogie carriages was purchased by the CLC permitting the replacement of 6-wheeled carriages in use on local services.

The last new coaches for the CLC were built by Cravens in 1937 to designs by Nigel (later Sir Nigel) Gresley. Of basically standard LNER pattern they comprised two trains of articulated stock in teak finish and ran, like all the best vehicles before them, on the Liverpool to Manchester service. With these carriages, the history of CLC rolling stock really comes to an end as the only further purchases were a few goods brake vans from the LNER in 1939 and 1940. After nationalisation the stock was dispersed and those coaches that had not been scrapped were renumberd into the London Midland Region 'M' series in the early 1950s. At the same time they lost their CLC livery — which had never varied from varnished teak for new coaches and painted oak brown for older ones (in both cases with the CLC crest on the carriage side) and were finished in the current British Railways colours.

## Stations

After Liverpool and Manchester Central stations, Southport Lord Street was the next largest terminal with Chester Northgate the smallest. Stockport Tiviot Dale was the largest through station, followed in size by Warrington and Northwich. Putting aside the grandeur of the two major terminals, then perhaps Lord Street was the most architecturally worthwhile. Fronting as it did the most important

street in Southport, stringent conditions regarding its design had been laid down by the local authorities. Fortunately it can still be seen today, though now it is in use as a bus station. Chester Northgate had little to commend it being dully built in red brick. It was demolished when a new road was built. On the other hand, Stockport Tiviot Dale, demolished soon after its last services were withdrawn, had with its slightly ecclesiastical frontage a great deal of charm. Warrington, as the principal intermediate station on the CLC main line, possessed a suitably imposing frontage rarely seen by passengers who normally entered from the street — a fact that has been recognised in the recent rebuilding. Northwich was rebuilt in 1897 in yellow brick and with much false gable over an intricately patterned iron canopy. Enough remains today to give an impression of how it looked when it was one of the busiest stations on the line.

The wayside stations followed several general designs according to their originating railway, but the influence of the MS&LR was notable in many cases. The three stations on ST&AJR (Cheadle, Northenden and Baguley) showed this clearly with their common building plan of one and two storey brick pavilions, with a single storey section in between — the steep roof brought forward on iron columns and shallow curved brackets to make a waiting shelter. On the opposite platform a simple open building known as a platform or side shed was provided. Decorative barge boards completed the picture as they did on similar stations on the 'new line' between Manchester and Liverpool. But here the barge boards were even more distinctive, varying in pattern, not only between stations but on different gables on the same building. As the years went by many of the side sheds had fireplaces installed and their open fronts blocked off with a wall and door. At the western end of the line, stations built by the G&LR were more elaborate and more individual to suit the tastes of the commuters from the fashionable residential districts which they served. With the new Merseyrail electrification, some of these stations have been bought back into use, and Cressington in particular has been so well restored as to win a Civic Trust Award.

The Cheshire Midland had its own style of Victorian Domestic architecture, stations being little more than a house with adjoining offices. Knutsford was built to a bigger scale and this included a circular brick water tower which, though other examples existed elsewhere on British railways, was the only one on the CLC. It was demolished when the station was modernised in 1979. The West Cheshire used a similar station but at Delamere and Mouldsworth, built in local sandstone in place of brick. The Southport and Cheshire Lines Extension had stations of both brick and wood, with several of the latter being very basic in their construction. Finally, stations on the North Liverpool Line showed traces of Domestic Revival styling, anticipating by some years the last practices of the Midland Railway.

If we include in our survey the particularly ornate barge boards of Baguley, Northenden and Cheadle signalboxes which have been said to have a flavour of the Great Northern Railway, then it can be stated with truth that somewhere or other on the CLC could be found architectural features of all three owning partners. There is, however, no doubt that the influence of the Manchester Sheffield and Lincolnshire Railway was the strongest and it is the one that can still be discerned today in some of the stations that remain.

## Signalling

As in other aspects of operation, signalling practice on the CLC was very individual. With its own works at Warrington until 1936, there were a number of noticeable special features. These included: large spectacles on the signal arms; lower quadrant signals standard until 1930 and when upper quadrant signals were introduced, these were 'of a naive style'; wood, lattice and after about 1920 concrete posts all with the distinctive CLC finial; arms very often mounted on both sides of the post to guard opposite tracks; use of multiple posts rather than brackets which led to massive structures. Similarly, with signalboxes of which about 130 were at one time in use the diversity was extreme but also, like the line itself, charming.

Perhaps the most appropriate epitaph for the Cheshire Lines Railway, its own preferred name, are the words of Gerald Leedham, the last Secretary and General Manager. Writing in 1945 he stated:

'Throughout the years of its history as a separate entity, the CLC has earned the goodwill of the public and has never brought discredit on its parent companies'.

Understated surely, like so much to do with the Cheshire Lines.

# Bibliography

Biddle, Gordon: *Victorian Stations*; David & Charles (Holdings) Ltd, 1973

Burton, Warwick R.: *Railways of Marple and District from 1794;* M. T. & W. R. Burton, 1980

Clarke, John: *Railways*; 2nd edition revised C. W. Heaps; Greater Manchester Council, 1976

Clough, David: *The Cheshire Lines Committee — past and present*; Railway World, September 1981

Daniels, G. and Dench L. A.: *Passengers No More*; Ian Allan Ltd, 1973 (2nd edition)

Dixon, F: *The Manchester South Junction and Altrincham Railway*; The Oakwood Press, 1973

Dow, George: *Great Central* (3 vols); Locomotive Publishing Co, 1959 onwards

Dow, George: *Midland Style*; Historical Model Railway Society, 1975

Ellis, C. Hamilton: *The Midland Railway*; Ian Allan Ltd, 1953

Freeman, T. W.: *The Conurbations of Great Britain*; Manchester University Press, 1959

Greville, M. D.: *Chronology of the Railways of Lancashire and Cheshire*; Railway and Canal Historical Society, 1981

Griffiths, R. P.: *The Cheshire Lines Railway*; The Oakwood Press, 1947, 1958 and 1978

Haresnape, Brian and Rowledge, Peter: *Robinson Locomotives*; Ian Allan Ltd, 1982

Hemingway, G. Y.: *The Coaching Stock of the Cheshire Lines Committee*; Historical Model Railway Society Library

Holt, G. O.: *North West*, Volume 10 of A Regional History of the Railways of Great Britain; David & Charles (Publishers) Ltd, 1978

Hunter, Loxton: *Wanderings in Lancashire and Cheshire, Official Guide of the Cheshire Lines Committee*; Eyre & Spottiswoode, 1896

Leedham, Gerald: *The Cheshire Lines Railway*; Railway Magazine, January and February 1945

Marshall, John: *Forgotten Railways: North-West England*; David & Charles (Publishers) Ltd, 1981

Owen, David: *The Manchester Ship Canal*; Manchester University Press, 1983

Platt, G. H.: *The Cheshire Lines Railway*; Historical Model Railway Society Journal, July 1967

Rush, R. W.: *British Steam Railcars*; The Oakwood Press, 1969

Wrottesley, John: *The Great Northern Railway* (2 Vols); B. T. Batsford, 1979

*Locomotives of the LNER* (15 vols published up to end 1983); The Railway Correspondence and Travel Society, 1963 onwards

*The ABC of British Railways Locomotives/Motive Power*; Ian Allan Ltd (various editions)

# Liverpool-Manchester

Four views at Liverpool Central station.

*Left:*
The 9.43am train from Gateacre stands under the arched roof on 24 October 1964.  *John Clarke*

*Top:*
The headquarters of the CLC photographed from Ranelagh Street at the turn of the last century. The top floor accommodated all the administrative staff of the railway for many years.
*County Down Museum Preservation Trust*

*Above right:*
Ex-LMS Stanier 2-6-4T No 42491 has its tanks filled at a fluted water column of standard CLC (GCR) type; 27 May 1963.  *I. G. Holt*

*Right:*
Ex-GCR LNER Class D9 4-4-0 No 2314 backs vigorously away from the platform end, closely watched by station staff; July 1949.  *F. Dean*

*Top:*
**MS&LR Class 14 2-2-2s were the first regular performers on the Liverpool-Manchester service. No 505 poses with its crew at Brunswick shed.**
*Real Photographs 16110*

*Above:*
**In later years GCR 4-4-0s monopolised the turn. As LNER D6 No 5871 stands in Brunswick shed yard with an LNER Class K3 2-6-0 in the background; August 1938.**
*W. Potter*

*Left:*
**GCR designs of 2-4-2T were used on local trains for many years, LNER Class F1 around Manchester and Class F2 around Liverpool. Unusually No 7100 of Class F1 is at Brunswick shed. The steps in the background were the means of entry from the road; 13 June 1948.**
*E. R. Wethersett Real Photographs 24645*

*Right:*
A general view of Brunswick shed in 1957 showing the smoky conditions that could be found. On view are locomotives Nos 42949, 65147, 63743 and two ex LMS 'Jinty' 0-6-0s. *J. A. Peden*

*Below:*
Brunswick Goods station on 4 April 1958. The warehouse built in 1893 dwarfs the original CLC passenger terminal of 1864. *J. A. Peden*

*Bottom:*
DMUs form the 14.57 Warrington-Liverpool Central, here passing Brunswick on 27 May 1963. In the distance is the abandoned Liverpool Overhead Railway tunnel entrance portal on the line to Dingle. The lines on the right run down to Herculaneum coal tips. *I. G. Holt*

*Above:*

**Stanier Class 5 4-6-0 No 44741, built in 1948 with Caprotti valve gear, blasts through St Michael's station with a train of oil tankers on 27 May 1963.** *I. G. Holt*

*Left:*

**Otterspool station looking towards Garston. The tall lattice post signal gives early sighting to engine drivers. Originally called Otters Pool, this station closed on 3 March 1951, earlier than others on the old G&LR.** *Collection of J. M. Ryan*

*Below:*

**Mersey Road and Aigburth station with a train about to leave in the direction of Garston. The CLC style of painting, alternate stripes of light and dark brown, can be seen on the platform canopies.** *Collection of J. M. Ryan*

*Above:*
**A Kirkby-Garston train formed of a pair of Class 503 EMUs runs into the newly-restored Cressington station on 30 June 1980. Services on this electrified Merseyrail line were extended to Hunts Cross on 16 May 1983.**
*J. G. Glover*

*Below:*
**A view of Garston station looking towards Manchester. The last coach of the local train is a 12-wheel brake 3rd built in 1880.** *Lens of Sutton*

*Top left:*
Hunts Cross station is now the interchange between the DMU service from Manchester, Oxford Road and the Merseyrail service to Kirkby. This old view shows the station building at road level.   *Collection of J. M. Ryan*

*Centre left:*
Steps from the roadbridge lead down to the platforms at Hunts Cross on 22 July 1957. Looking towards Liverpool from the main line platforms, the road level station buildings are on the left with the Southport line platforms far right. The CLC cast iron 'Gents' was found at several other locations.   *J. A. Peden*

*Bottom left:*
Halewood Sidings when they were a hive of activity. The driver checks the motion of No 63612 an ex-LNER Class O4/8 (the rebuild of Robinson GCR 2-8-0s using a

'B1' class boiler). In the foreground is the Liverpool-Manchester main line. Photo taken 28 March 1959.
*J. A. Peden*

*Above:*
A through train from Liverpool Central to the GCR hauled by one of that company's 4-4-0s No 1040 (later LNER Class D9) passes Halewood station c1910. The circles on the signal arms denote those controlling entry to the goods lines inside Halewood triangle.
*H. Gordon-Tidey Collection of H. C. Casserley*

*Below:*
The last green fields before the suburbs of Liverpool. A pair of Derby two-car DMUs make up the 2.30pm Manchester Central-Liverpool Central near Hough Green on 15 March 1963.   *I. G. Holt*

Photographs taken by H. Gordon-Tidey between Halewood and Hough Green show some of the motive power usual on the CLC mainline around 1910.

*Top left:*
**GCR Sacré Class 6B 4-4-0 No 438 (later LNER Class D12) heads a mixed train which includes a cattle truck.**
*Locomotive & General 7564*

*Centre left:*
**A Midland Railway 'Spinner' 4-2-2 No 622 heads a Derby-Southport express. A batch of these engines was based on the Midland shed at Brunswick to work their through traffic over the CLC. The first coach is an early Midland 12-wheeler.**
*Collection of H. C. Casserley*

*Bottom left:*
**GCR Pollitt 4-2-2 No 970 built at Gorton in 1900 and here seen with a Robinson chimney, hauls a set of Gresley designed carriages, built for the Liverpool-Manchester service in 1911.** *Collection of J. M. Ryan*

*Above:*
**Midland Railway 4-4-0 No 330 (with an extended smoke box) heads a through train of Midland carriages.**
*Real Photographs 41079*

*Right:*
**The ganger walks his stretch of line as GCR Pollitt Class 11a 4-4-0 No 854 (later LNER Class D6) passes with an express.** *IAL*

*Above:*
**One of the 0-6-0s Parker designed for the MS&LR, ex-LNER Class J10 No 65128, approaches Farnworth from the Manchester direction at the head of a special train on 6 June 1949. The white sighting board behind the distant signal arm is there to make it easier to see against the embankment side.** *R. E. Gee*

*Below:*
**In British Railways lined black livery, ex-LMS Class 2P 4-4-0 No 40396 leaves Farnworth on a Manchester-Liverpool express on 6 June 1949. The concrete bridge in the left background was built when the tunnel at this point was opened out in the early 1920s.** *R. E. Gee*

*Below right:*
**Sankey station looking towards Manchester.** *Warrington Museum and Art Gallery.*

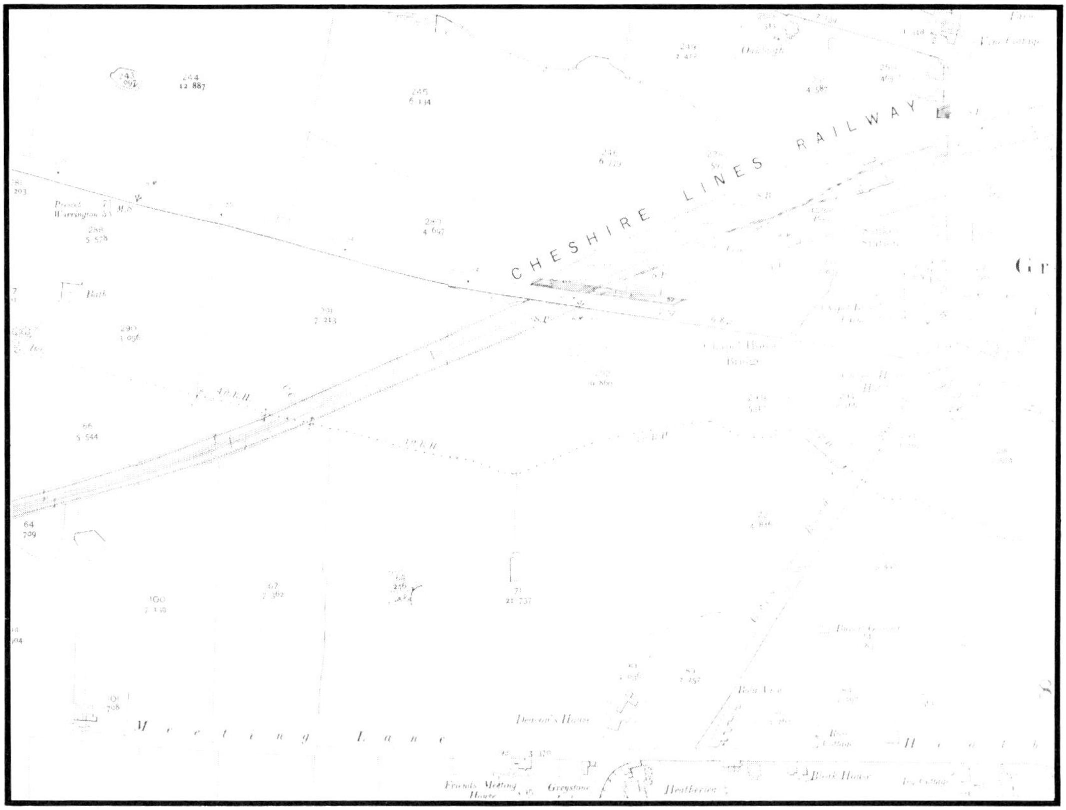
CHESHIRE LINES RAILWAY
Meeting Lane

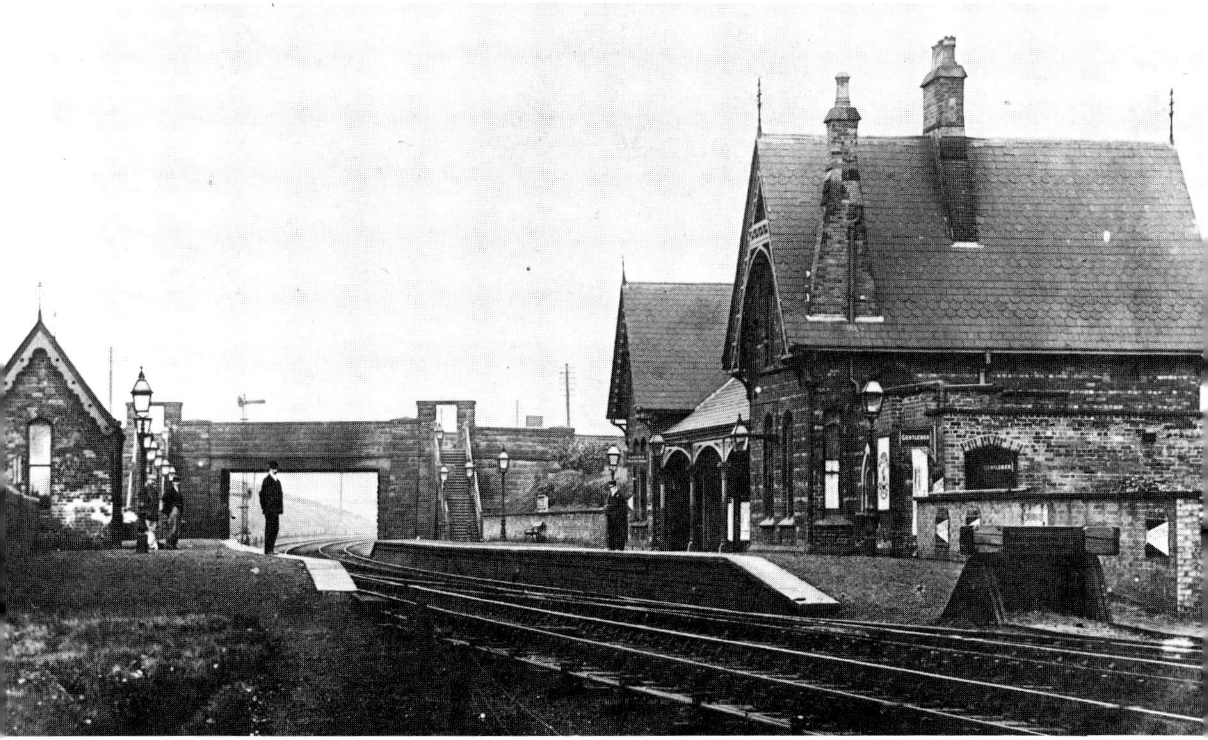
GENTLEMEN

*Above:*
**An ex-LMS Fowler 2-6-4T heads a Nottingham-Liverpool express over Froghall Lane bridge in Warrington. c1958.** *Peter Norton*

*Right:*
**Drinking fountains were a feature of stations on the CLC main line, but differed in detail. No longer in working order, they have been variously decorated — this one at Warrington Central station with the date of nationalisation and a BR speed arrow; 19 July 1983.** *N. F. W. Dyckhoff*

*Below:*
**Warrington Goods Warehouse c1960.** *Alan Bryant*

*Above:*
New buildings at street level were opened in 1983 and include a single ticket barrier to replace two separate platform entrances. The old building can be seen at the rear; 19 September 1983. *Richard Fox*

*Below:*
Trains pass at Warrington Central on 15 May 1959. Facing towards Manchester is an ex-LMS Stanier 2-6-2T No 40094 while one of Stanier's 2-6-4Ts, No 42612, heads the Liverpool train. *J. A. Peden*

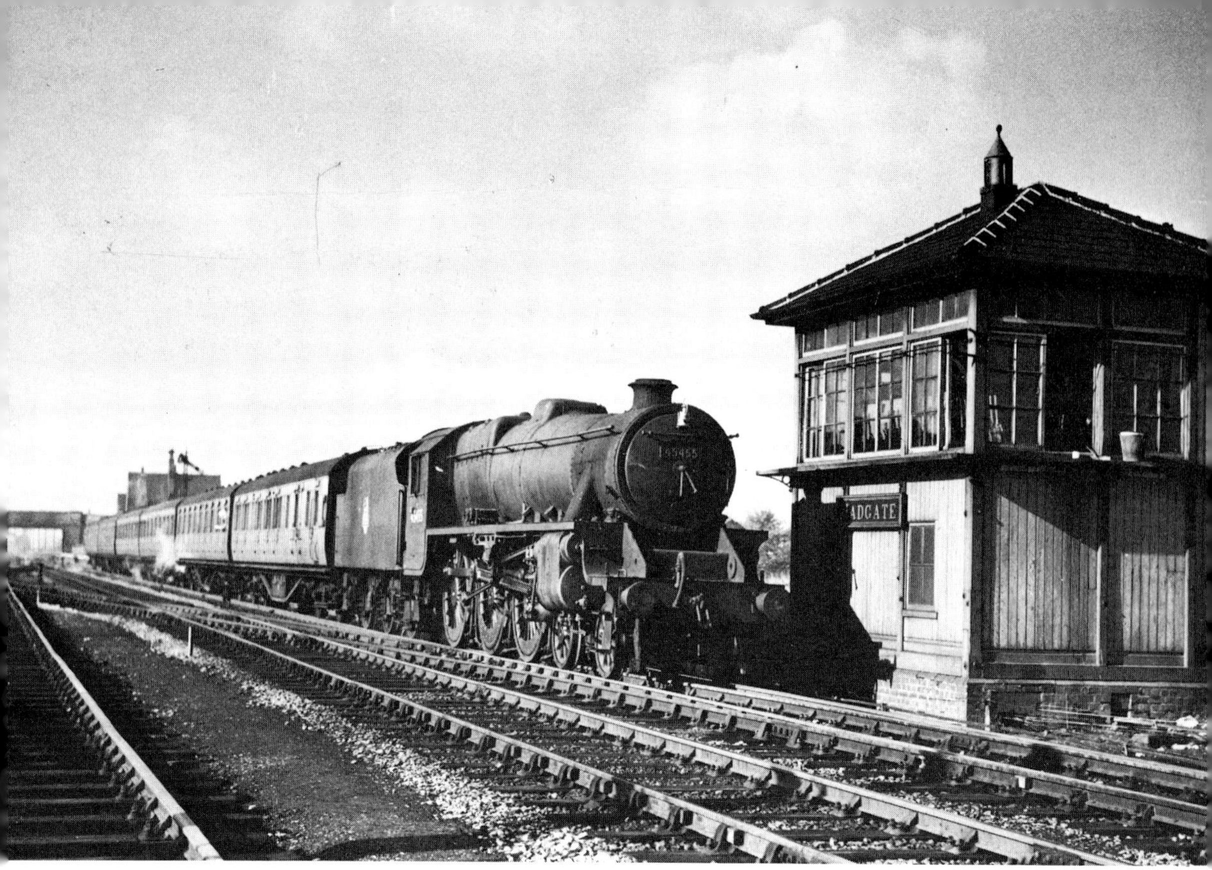

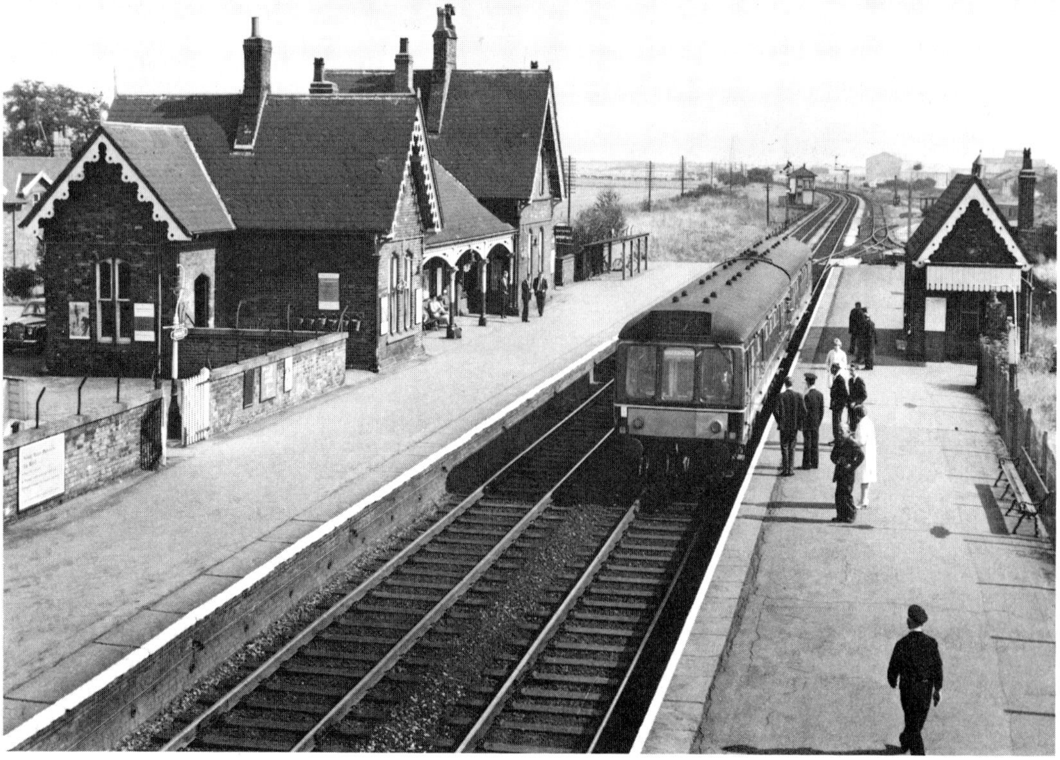

*Top left:*

**The 10.10am (SO) stopping train from Warrington to Stockport passes Padgate signalbox hauled by ex-LMS Stanier Class 5 4-6-0 No 45455. Note the distinctive ventilator on the signalbox; 17 October 1953.**
*E. D. Bruton*

*Below left:*

**Eleven years later, the opposite working, the 11.40am (SO) Stockport Tiviot Dale-Warrington Central train is greeted by the station master as it draws to a halt at Padgate station. The waste ground at the end of the up platform used to hold the ballast sidings that served the CLC; 12 September 1964.** *N. F. W. Dyckhoff*

*Right:*

**Risley Moss lives up to its reputation as the signalbox gradually subsides into the peat. The lineside hut and gradient post are also typical CLC; 14 January 1962.**
*Peter Norton*

*Inset:*

**Commemorative plaque to mark the opening of Birchwood station by Sir Peter Parker MVO.** *N. F. W. Dyckhoff*

*Below:*

**An afternoon DMU for Hunts Cross slips into Birchwood during 1983. The station stands close to the site of Risley station opened in 1940 to cater for a wartime Royal Ordnance Factory, and which closed in 1952.**
*N. F. W. Dyckhoff*

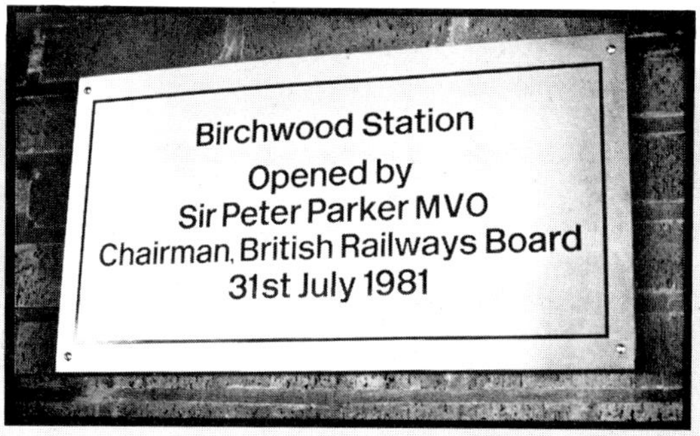

Birchwood Station
Opened by
Sir Peter Parker MVO
Chairman, British Railways Board
31st July 1981

*Top left:*
Ex-GER LNER Class D16/3 4-4-0 No 62535 ran trials on
the CLC from late 1949 to early 1950. Liked by
enginemen, the 'Claud' was joined by seven more and all
except one were stationed at Trafford Park. They stayed
on the CLC until 1952, latterly working Chester trains.
Here the locomotive heads the 1.30pm Liverpool-
Manchester Sunday train approaching Glazebrook and
composed of Gresley designed articulated stock on
19 March 1950.  *J. D. Darby*

*Centre left:*
The same service, again with articulated stock on
31 December 1955. Stanier 2-6-2T No 40203 runs its train
through Glazebrook West Jn. The line to Wigan and
St Helens bears off to the right.  *R. W. Hinton*

*Below left:*
With Dam Lane Jn in the background, ex-LMS
Compound 4-4-0 No 41082 heads a Grand National
special on 25 March 1950.  *J. D. Darby*

*Right:*
Glazebrook West Jn signalbox, one of the tall brick-built
type. The signal on the left has replacement LMS type
posts and arms on a CLC bracket base; 22 May 1959.
*Peter Norton*

*Below:*
No 42050, first of the ex-LMS Fairburn 2-6-4Ts, enters
Glazebrook with the 5.12pm Manchester-Liverpool train
on 28 August 1964. The station cottages are prominent
behind the down platform.  *N. F. W. Dyckhoff*

*Above:*
**Stanier 2-6-4T No 42479 heads a train towards Glazebrook East Jn on 30 March 1958.** *Peter Norton*

*Left:*
Looking down on the Manchester Ship Canal Company line, leading to Partington coaling basin and laid on the old track bed of the CLC between Glazebrook and Partington. The new course of this line is on the right running up to Cadishead Viaduct over the canal. No D14, an MSC Co Hudswell Clark 0-6-0 diesel mechanical locomotive shunts empties alongside a train of steel bars from BSC (Irlam) in June 1977. *D. Thorpe*

Turning east shows the face of the signal — a fine example of a CLC upper quadrant bracket with a pair of small central arms. These control the goods sidings in between the Manchester main line to the left and the Skelton Jn line to the right. A post marking the boundary of the Liverpool division is at the base of the signal. Photo taken 30 March 1958. *Peter Norton*

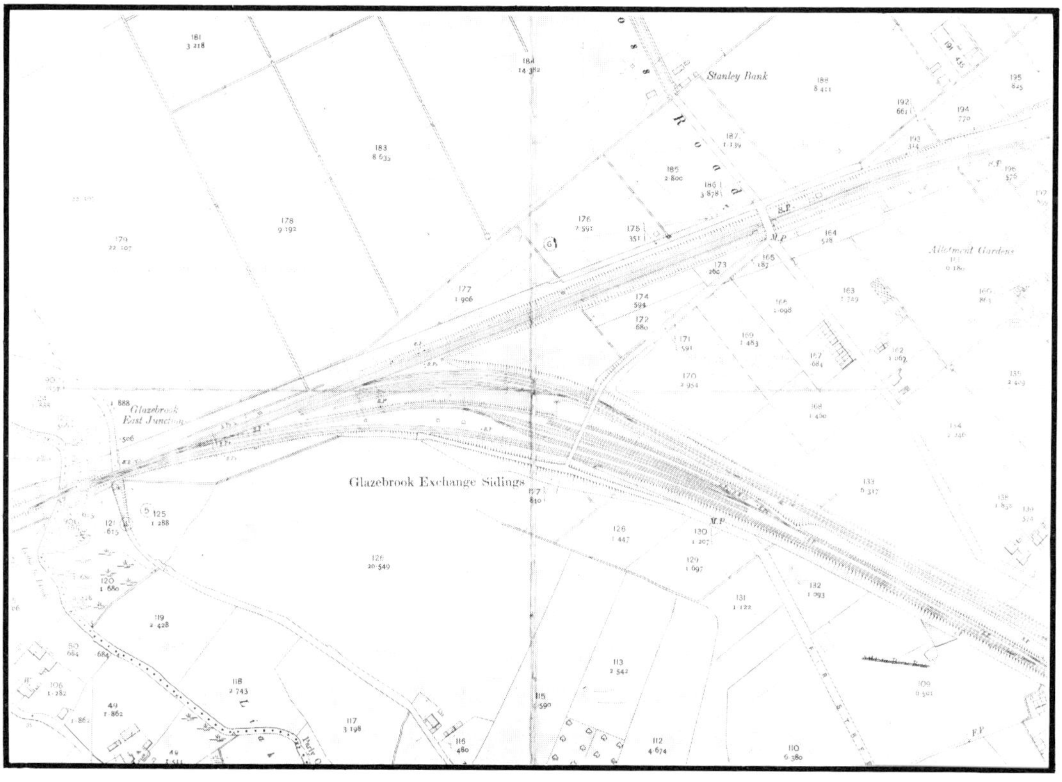

When the Manchester Ship Canal was built, the CLC also had to be diverted between Irlam and Flixton — Deviation No 5. The course of the line changed through Irlam for Cadishead station and this required the station to be rebuilt on a new site. Unfortunately the line of the Deviation itself was then altered and wide platforms were needed to link with the new station building. A covered awning was also provided. This view was taken in July 1939. *R. F. Roberts*

A scene of human activity as the bed of the Manchester Ship Canal is dug out by hand c1892. Irlam Viaduct is complete and in use, the spoil from the Ship Canal having been used to construct the embankments so that services on the CLC between Liverpool and Manchester would not be interrupted. Unfortunately, when the canal was filled, the main piers settled causing the brick arches to become unsafe. They were replaced by the steel spans seen in the modern photograph. *MSC Co*

The DMU forming the 11.12am local train from Warrington Central to Manchester, Oxford Road leaves Irlam Viaduct on 4 October 1980 at the point where the River Mersey enters the canal. Like the similar one at Cadishead, on the line from Glazebrook East Jn to Skelton Jn the bridge was built to accommodate four tracks, although the embankments were only made wide enough for two. This was the most cost effective way for the MSC Co to allow for the possible future traffic needs of the CLC, as once the canal had been filled, extra tracks would have required another bridge and supporting embankments. *David Clough*

URMSTON. C.L.C.

*Above:*
**Commuters line the platform as a train for Manchester approaches Urmston station c1905.** *Lens of Sutton*

*Below:*
**Urmston station approach.**
*Manchester Polytechnic, Manchester Studies Unit*

*Above:*
Fortunately the CLC has suffered very few accidents. But on 11 December 1958 between Urmston and Trafford Park the 5.30pm Liverpool-Manchester express made up of seven non-corridor coaches and hauled by Fairburn 2-6-4T No 42184 came to grief. A crane engaged in culvert making had over-balanced and fallen down the embankment. Speed was estimated at 60 to 65mph and although reduced prior to impact the locomotive was derailed when it struck the crane's bucket and jib.
*C. C. Ashton, Collection of R. G. Chapman*

*Below:*
Part of the CLC line has been electrified at the Manchester end to enable through trains to reach Trafford Park freightliner terminal and also to allow EMUs to operate football specials to the halt at Old Trafford football ground — home of Manchester United. Here, the 17.57 Oxford Road-Liverpool Lime Street service is approaching Old Trafford station in July 1980. The 25kV catenary is clearly visible as is the remodelled junction to Throstle Nest curve on the right. *Richard Fox*

*Top:*
Trafford Park was the largest shed on the CLC. This interior view taken in June 1933 shows ex-GER LNER 'J69' 0-6-0T No 7273 and a number of ex-GCR LNER Class C13 4-4-2Ts. Four 'J69s' were at this shed in 1935 and worked at Deansgate goods depot and as goods pilot at Manchester Central. *W. Potter*

*Above:*
Ex-GNR LNER Class C12 4-4-2T No 4517, one of four shedded at Trafford Park when this photograph was taken in 1945. They had arrived during the war and found use on local services from Manchester Central to Guide Bridge, Wigan, Warrington and Chester (a run on which the

enginemen particularly disliked them). Two stayed on and worked as passenger pilot at Central station for a time. *W. Potter*

*Above:*
Class 13 4-4-2T No 5453 hangs from the locomotive crane inside the shed; August 1936. *W. Potter*

*Below:*
A view over the Rochdale Canal at Castlefield, 12 March 1966. The lower line is the MSJ&AR to Oxford Road, the higher line is the CLC approach to Manchester Central. *H. D. Bowtell*

A sad change from the splendours of the past. The
magnificent roof remains as does the ornate clock case
made by the CLC themselves, but the 13.37 Liverpool
train is now a DMU and the noise and bustle of the once
busy terminal have gone; November 1967.
*K. Groundwater*

*Left:*
'Director' class locomotives played a major role on Chester line services in the 1950s. Ex-GCR LNER Class D10 4-4-0 No 62650 *Prince Henry* stands at the head of the 12.30pm (SO) train to Northwich on 4 April 1953. The scaffolding is in place for the reglazing of Central station roof which took place at this time. *W. Potter*

*Below:*
Another ex-GCR locomotive LNER Class B2 4-6-0, No 5427 *City of London* seen in July 1937. In the right background can be seen Deansgate goods warehouse built by the Great Northern Railway and served by a short branch from the main line. One of the first major steel-framed brick-panelled buildings in Britain, it was completed in 1898. *W. Potter*

*Bottom:*
Carrying its new number under the short-lived LNER renumbering scheme, engine No 2319 of Class D9 stands at the head of its train and ready to depart from Central station on 30 August 1947. *J. D. Darby*

*Above:*
The classic view of Manchester Central. The station closed on 5 May 1969, last services having run the Saturday before. Now gutted, and after use as a car park, it awaits resurrection as an exhibition hall. *British Rail*

*Below:*
MS&LR Class 24 2-4-0 No 57 stands in the station c1901. Built at Gorton in 1867 and scrapped in 1903, it spent many years shedded at Northwich. It is reputed to have hauled the first train from there into Manchester Central when the new station opened on 1 July 1880. The pipes on the side of the smoke box were fitted as part of the Smiths simple vacuum brake system used on the CLC. *Collection of W. Egerton*

43

# Chester-Altrincham

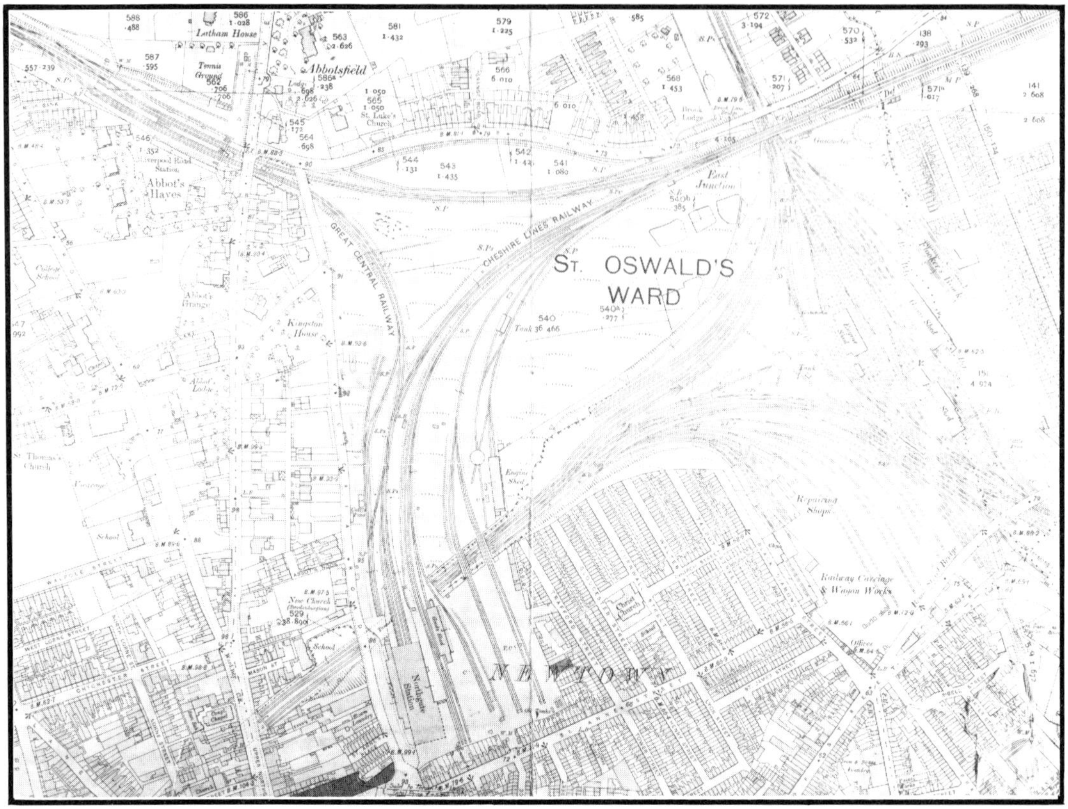

Passenger services started to Chester Northgate from Manchester Oxford Road on 1 May 1875. The engine shed was probably erected at that time. Originally it was a sub shed of Northwich and this seems to have continued until about 1923. The shed closed to steam on 4 January 1960 and Northgate station shut on 6 October 1969 when trains were re-routed to Chester General.

*Below:*
Chester had an allocation of LNER Class N5 0-6-2Ts from their introduction in 1923. Now Class N5/2 No 69293 stands outside its home shed, 20 August 1955. *Brian Morrison*

*Right:*
**In simplified livery, NE on the tender, No 2101 of
Class D6, one of the few to receive its new LNER number
(mounted low to avoid the brass beading) stands by the the
coaling stage on 24 April 1947. It was withdrawn at the
end of the year.** *H. C. Casserley*

*Below:*
**Stanier 2-6-2T No 40209 stands at the shed door in March
1953. Behind the turntable on the right an old CLC coach
body serves as a shed.** *Real Photographs K1747*

*Bottom:*
**Ex-LNER Class D11/1 4-4-0 No 62661** *Gerard Powys
Dewhirst* **one of Robinson's large 'Director' development
of Class D10 waits to leave Chester Northgate for
Manchester Central on 20 August 1955.** *Brian Morrison*

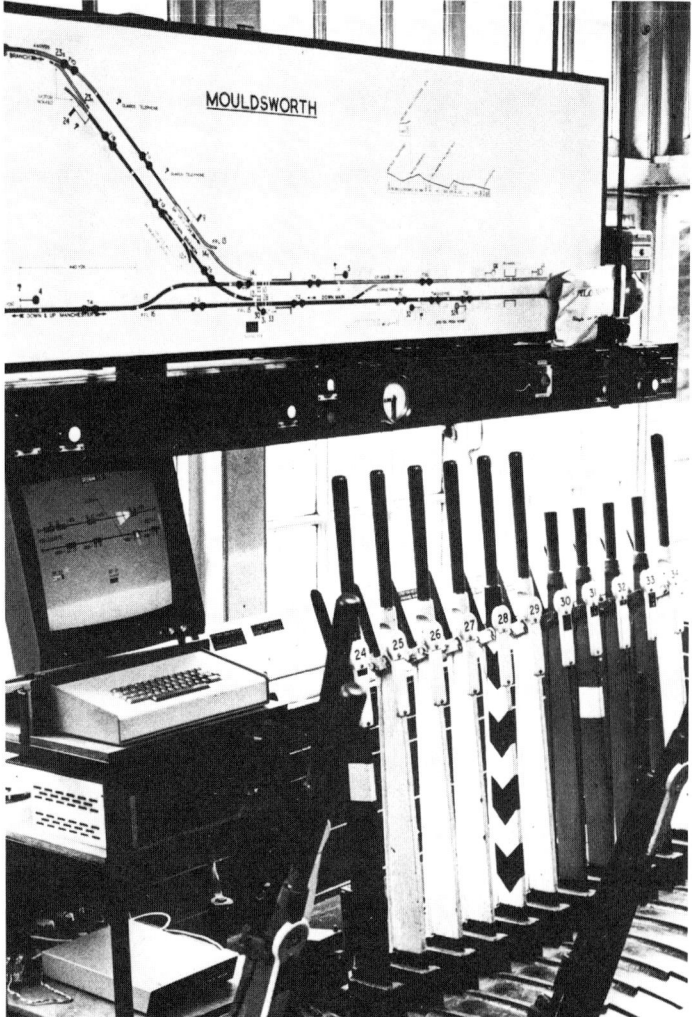

*Above left:*
**Barrow for Tarvin station closed from
1 June 1953. D11/1 No 62661** *Gerard
Powys Dewhirst* **heads the 2.45pm
Chester Northgate to Manchester
Central train on the station's last day
of services, 30 May 1953. The deserted
platforms tell their own story. Built at
the same time as the CLC Liverpool-
Manchester main line was under
construction, its design was the same
as the stations on that line.**
*R. H. Hughes*

*Left:*
**Mouldsworth signalbox dates from
around 1903. Now much modernised
internally it uses three types of control
— token, tokenless and normal block.
Photo taken 20 July 1983.**
*N. F. W. Dyckhoff*

*Right:*
**A Class 40 comes off the single line
section from West Cheshire Jn and the
second man surrenders the token to the
Mouldsworth signalman. The line
sweeping left also reverts to single line
and reaches Chester General by way of
Mickle Trafford Jn.** *David Clough*

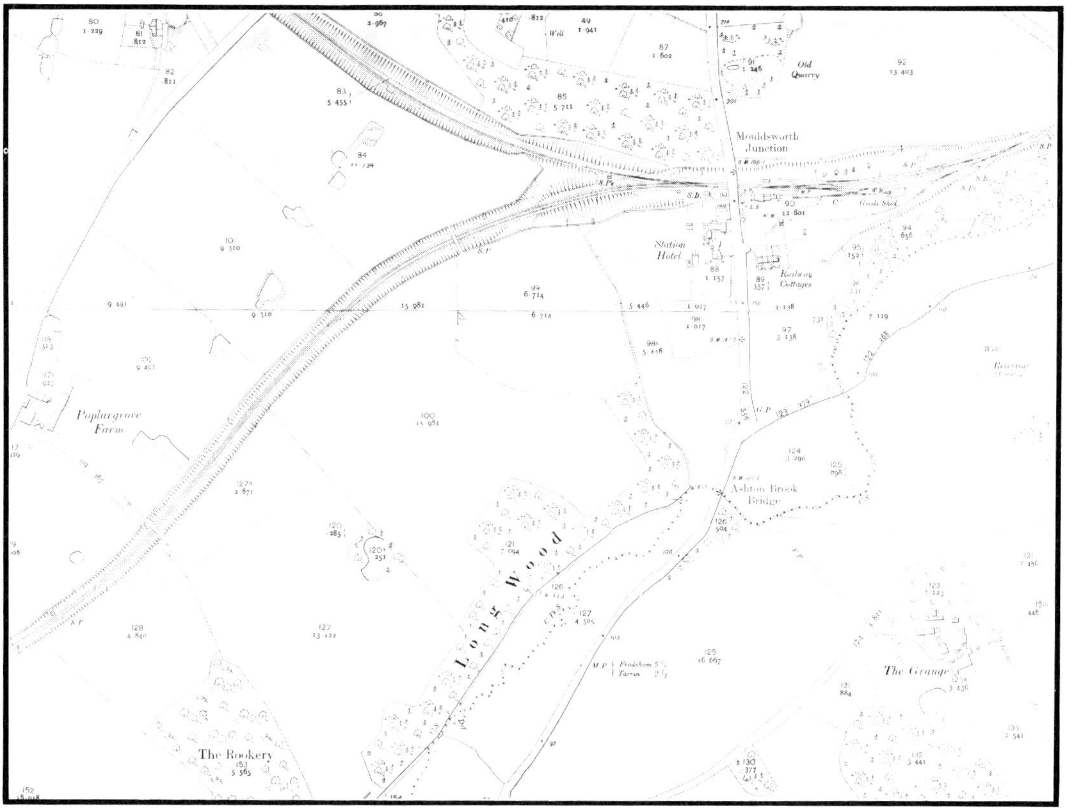
Mouldsworth Junction
Old Quarry
Well
Station Hotel
Railway Cottages
Goods Shed
Poplargrove Farm
Long Wood
Ashton Brook Bridge
The Rookery
The Grange

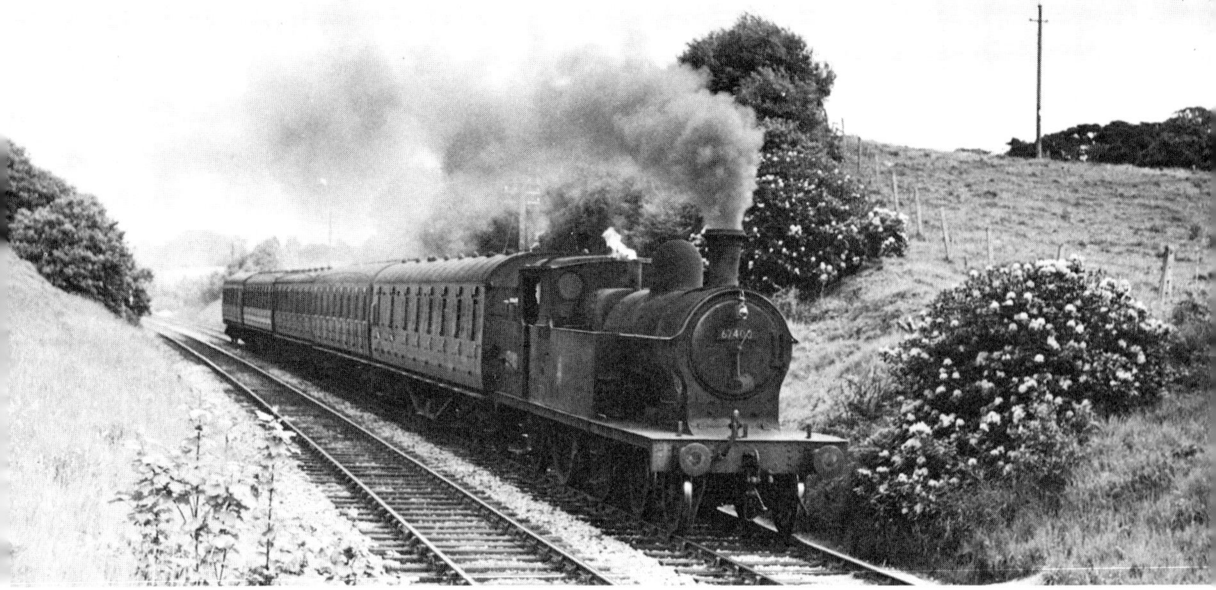

*Above:*
**Rhododendrons bloom at the trackside as Class C13 4-4-2T No 67400 heads a Chester train between Delamere and Mouldsworth, on 16 June 1951.**
*J. F. Russell-Smith NRM (Crown Copyright)*

*Left:*
**Railwaymen pose for their photograph on Delamere station built, like Mouldsworth, in local red sandstone. Milk churns and a hen pecking at the platform surface are no longer seen today with Delamere an unstaffed halt and the buildings boarded up.**
*Collection J. M. Ryan*

*Below left:*
**The inhabitants stand outside Delamere railway cottages, brick built and now demolished. The closeness of the goods siding is noticeable.**
*Collection of J. M. Ryan*

*Right:*
**Delamere signalbox is still in good condition in 1966. A shunters pole leans against the concrete signal post which shows serious corrosion. The distinctive CLC lower quadrant arm with green and red glasses of equal size is clearly seen as is the CLC finial.**
*W. A. Corkhill*

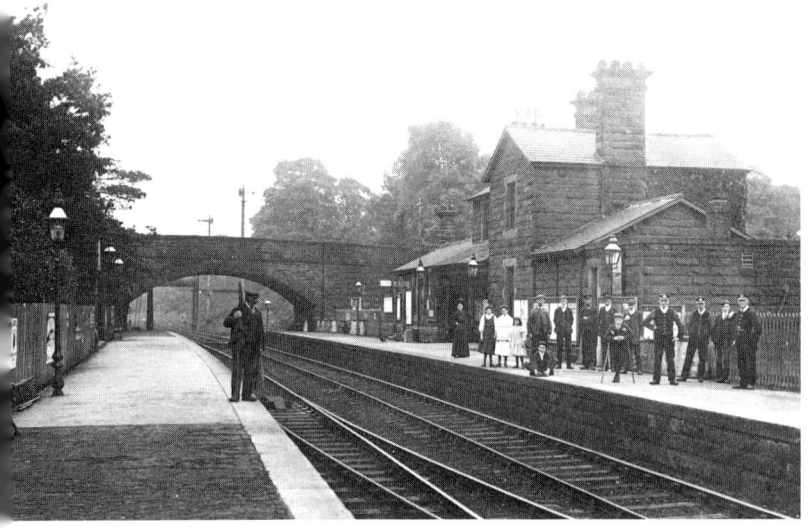

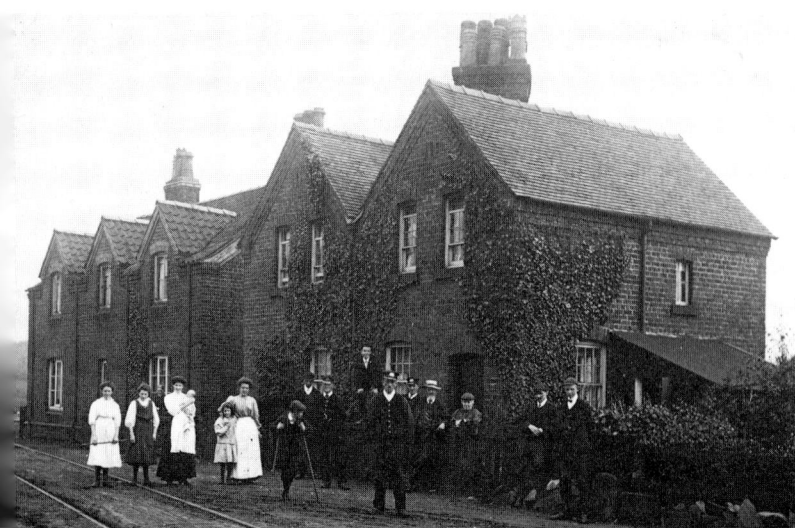

CHESHIRE LINES RAILWAY
Government Cottages
Linmer Cottage
Delamere Station
Crane
D E L A

DELAMERE

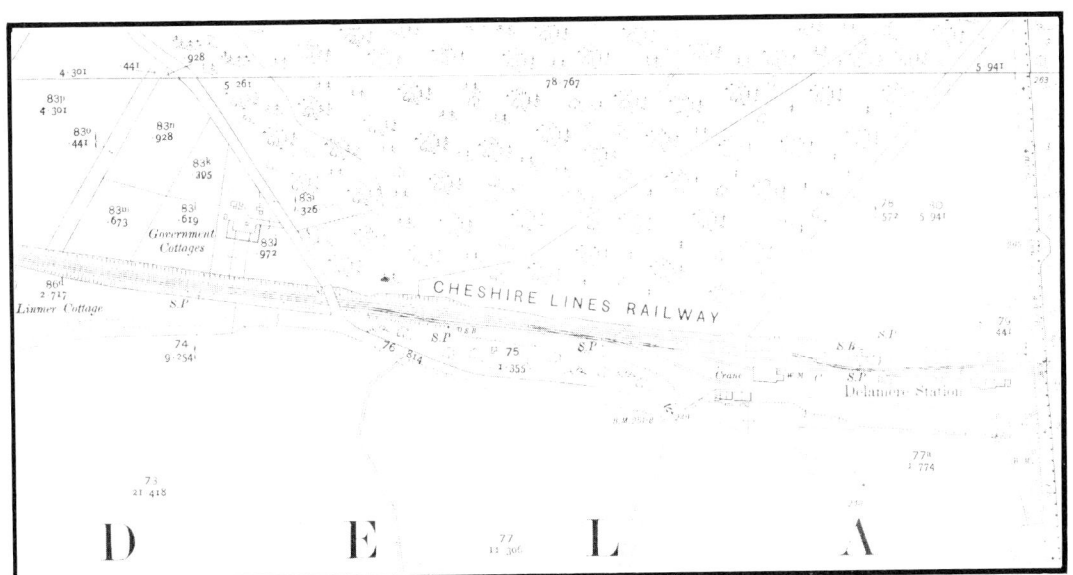

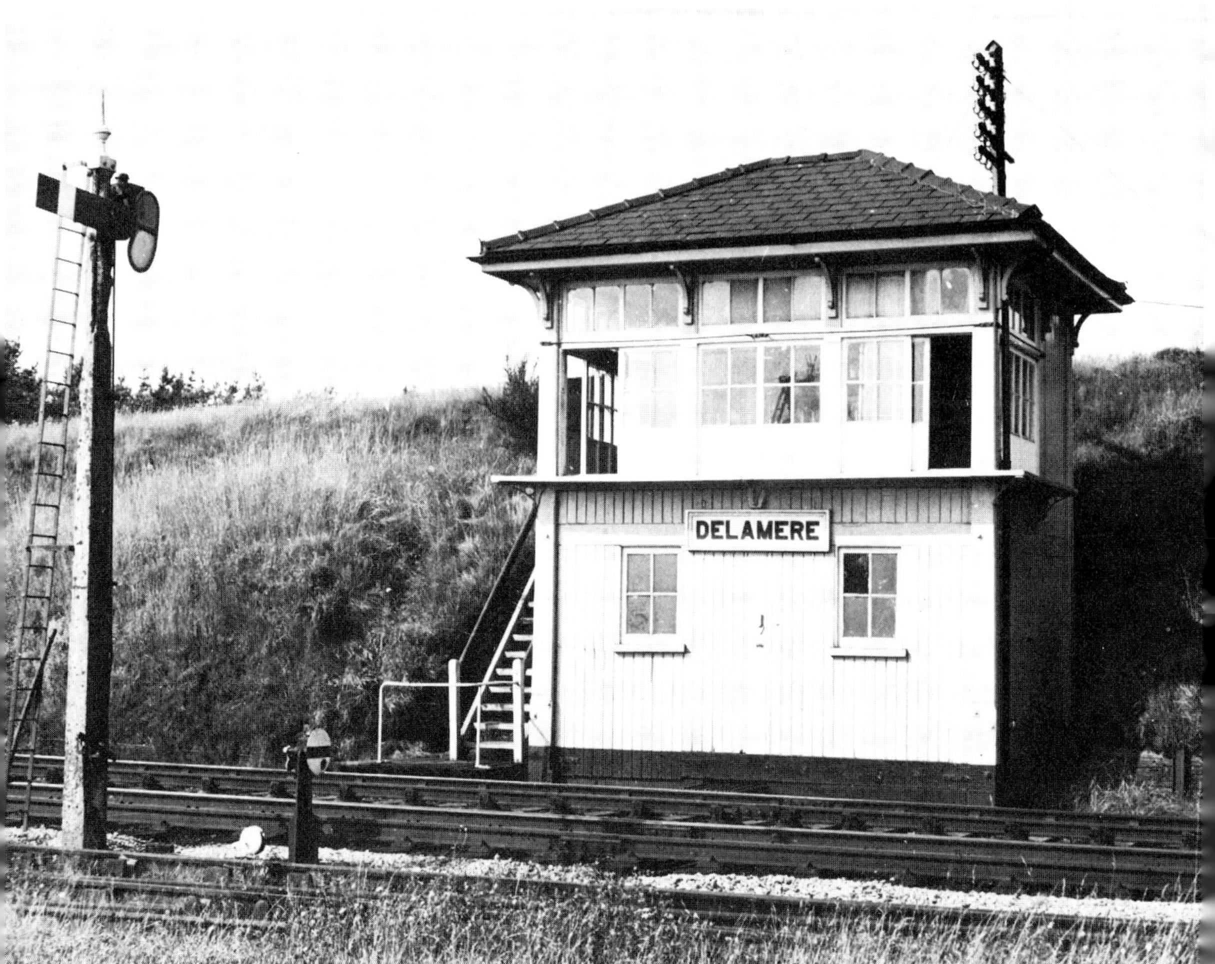

Class 04/8 2-8-0 No 63802, British Railways in full on the tender, breasts the summit in the heart of Delamere forest with a down freight on 10 May 1949. *P. M. Alexander*

View of the goods yard from Cuddington signalbox in 1904. A pair of Sacré 0-6-0 locomotives stand side by side — a salt truck is coupled behind the right-hand engine. *M. Witte. Author's Collection*

*Above:*
**A DMU bound for Chester crosses the new bridge near Hartford which carries the CLC over the West Coast main line; 19 July 1983.** *N. F. W. Dyckhoff*

*Inset:*
**Class 40 No 40.079 creeps down from Hartford CLC Jn and approaches the junction with the West Coast Main line, 19 July 1983.** *N. F. W. Dyckhoff*

*Below:*
**The 11.28 Chester General-Manchester Oxford Road DMU approaches Hartford CLC Jun on 19 July 1983 — the line taken by the train above can be seen bearing right.** *N. F. W. Dyckhoff*

*Top:*
**LNER Class J39 0-6-0 No 64745 accelerates its freight train through Hartford and Greenbank in 1951. The station has changed very little over the years except in name. It is now called simply Greenbank to avoid confusion with the nearby Hartford station on the Crewe-Liverpool Lime Street line.** *N. F. W. Dyckhoff*

*Above:*
**Two Robinson 2-6-4Ts LNER Class L3 worked at Hartford exchange sidings from 1943 until withdrawn. The engines were employed banking goods trains over the short branch to the ICI plant at Winnington Park and on trips between Winnington and Northwich. No 69052 lasted longest, going in 1954. This photo taken 21 March 1953.** *N. Fields*

*Below:*
*Joule* a Peckett saddle tank built in 1897 poses with driver, shunters and foreman in the sidings serving Brunner Mond & Co's Lostock Works in 1915. A Midland 0-6-4T stands behind. *ICI Mond Division*

*Above:*
Trucks carrying deliveries of limestone from the Peak District and coal from North Staffordshire stand at Winnington Works in pre-Grouping days. A Caledonian Railway wagon is tucked between Midland and Cheshire Lines examples, while a Sacré Class 18 0-6-0 shunts in the distance. *ICI Mond Division*

One of the most important engineering works on the CLC is the viaduct between Hartford and Northwich which carries the railway over the rivers Dane and Weaver and the Weaver Canal. It consists of 48 stone arches and two wrought iron girder bridges giving a total length of around 725 yards. Its condition now causes concern.

*Above and Below left:*
**DMUs forming the Chester-Manchester service cross the viaduct on 23 February 1983.** *G. W. Morrison*

*Below:*
**Picked out in silhouette, an LMS Class 4F 0-6-0 No 4284 heads a mineral train across the viaduct in 1934.** *Douglas Barnard*

*Above:*
The CLC, like other railways after World War 1 started to use reinforced concrete for lineside fittings. This footbridge was erected in 1922 as indicated by the CLR monogram. Although damaged, it still stands outside Northwich. This recent photograph was taken on 20 July 1983.
*N. F. W. Dyckhoff*

*Below:*
Class 40 No 40.035 leaves Northwich with its ICI stone train from Tunstead on 28 October 1983, having picked up a banker (hidden behind the footbridge) for the 1 in 53 climb up to Oakleigh sidings. This is one of the last regular workings for banking engines in the northwest. The line to the right was put in during World War 2 to join the Northwich to Middlewich line of the LMS. *Steve Turner*

*Below:*
**Northwich station frontage c1908.** *Collection of W. Egerton*

*Bottom:*
**In 1966 a fine pair of CLC lower quadrant signals on concrete posts and with shunting and calling-on arms stand at the east end of Northwich station platform. Ex-LMS Stanier Class 8F 2-8-0 No 48693 passes its home shed with a down mixed goods.** *W. A. Corkhill*

*Top left:*
Northwich shed has hosted preserved locomotives since the ban on steam working was lifted by British Rail. LMS Class 5 No 5000 from the Severn Valley Railway receives attention before proceeding to Bold Colliery to take part in the 'Rocket 150' celebrations, 19 April 1980.  *Bob Avery*

*Inset left:*
The shed in 1952. Locomotives that can be identified include Class J10 No 65131, Class D10 No 62651 and Class J39S No 64901. On the right is the covered coaling stage.  *Locomotive & General 26486*

*Bottom left:*
Lifting sheerlegs were provided at the main CLC sheds. Here on 20 August 1955 'D10' 4-4-0 No 62653 *Sir Edward Fraser* the last of the class to be withdrawn in October of this year, hangs suspended.  *Brian Morrison*

*Above right:*
Plumley, typical of the brick-built Cheshire Midland stations, had its name changed from Plumbley in 1944. Looking towards Manchester, this 15 June 1952 view is full of interesting detail: 5ton crane, cycle shed, North Western bus timetable case, fishboxes, all evidence that this immaculately kept station is alive and well-used.
*J. D. Darby*

*Below:*
Pictures of trains taken moving away from the photographer are sadly rare. This excellent example shows the crew of ex-GCR LNER Class J10 0-6-0 No 5194 at work on the footplate as their Manchester-bound train approaches Knutsford.
*J. F. Russell-Smith NRM (Crown Copyright)*

The Railway Station — Knutsford

*Above:*
**GCR Pollitt Class 11A 4-4-0 No 872
leaves Knutsford with a Manchester to
Wrexham train c1910. Immediately
behind the engine are two GCR
through coaches for Aberystwyth via
Chester Liverpool Road.**
*H. Gordon-Tidey, Real Photographs
65328*

*Left:*
**Knutsford station looking in the
direction of Manchester c1910; note
circular water tower on the right.**
*Collection of J. M. Ryan*

*Above:*
The first big outing for Altrincham children was arranged by a local cinema manager who, in 1909, took 1,000 on a special train to Mobberley. The forerunner of many similar picnics, this one was filmed for later showing at the regular Saturday matinee. A still from the film shows supervisors and children at the start of the day.
*Borough of Trafford Library Service*

*Right:*
Mobberley station with CLC railwayman's house.
*Collection of J. M. Ryan*

*Above left:*
**Ashley was a favourite location for photographers, being easily accessible from South Manchester. 'J10' 0-6-0 No 5166 and 'N5' 0-6-2T No 69281, an unusual combination, head a mixed goods on 26 June 1948.** *J. D. Darby*

*Centre left:*
**The down platform with side shed and name board 'Ashley for Rostherne'. A large number of CLC stations displayed names 'for' somewhere else nearby. Photo taken 15 June 1952.** *J. D. Darby*

*Bottom left:*
**Wartime allotments by the track at Ashley were kept cultivated by the occupants of the railway cottages. A BR standard 2-6-4T passes with a Chester-Manchester train. Rarely seen on the CLC, a few of these locomotives were stationed at Chester between 1956 and 1960.** *R. H. Hughes*

*Top right:*
**Renumbered LNER Class J11 0-6-0 No 4382 (old No 5254) leaves Ashley with the 5.08pm Manchester-Chester train of seven carriages on 3 May 1947.** *J. D. Darby*

*Centre right:*
**The same train on 9 August 1947, again with seven carriages, leaves Ashley hauled by LNER Class B7 4-6-0 No 1397. This engine was the last of the class to be built in 1924 and like the rest a not infrequent visitor to the CLC.** *J. D. Darby*

*Bottom right:*
**An ex-GCR Robinson 'Glenalmond', LNER Class B8, No 1357 *Earl Roberts of Kandahar* approaches Ashley on a goods train for Northwich on 26 June 1948.** *J. D. Darby*

Guarding the down line into Hale station stands the last
CLC lattice signal. It replaced a wooden posted signal as
recently as 1951. Said to be destined for the National
Railway Museum in York, it now carries LMS type upper
quadrant arms. Class 40 No 40.099 passes with a train of
loaded ICI hopper wagons on 21 July 1983.
*N. F. W. Dyckhoff*

*Above:*
Hale station opened 12 May 1862 and was then called
Bowden Peel Causeway. It was renamed Peel Causeway
Bowden soon afterwards and then became Peel Causeway,
probably in 1881. Finally it was named Hale in 1902. A
busy commuter station, it has remained architecturally
unspoiled to the present day. The chimney in the
background belonged to Hale brewery and was demolished
in 1907 — dating the picture as the early years of this
century. *Lens of Sutton*

*Below:*
Altrincham and Bowden new combined station opened
3 April 1881. This junction marked the beginning of the
CLC track to Chester. Stanier 2-8-0 No 48017 storms by
on 8 June 1964 with a limestone train while a MSJ&AR
electric train, composed of a three car set with Motor
Brake Second M28571M waits to leave for Manchester
Oxford Road. The electric service on 1,500V DC began on
11 May 1931 and was withdrawn on 3 May 1971 when the
25kV system was extended from Oxford Road.
*N. F. W. Dyckhoff*

# Glazebrook-Godley Junction

*Above:*
**Withdrawal notices are posted on the board outside the entrance as Cadishead station sees out its last day of services, 28 November 1964.** *R. H. Hughes*

*Below:*
**The CLC replaced many wooden station nameboards with this pattern made in reinforced concrete. Photo taken 13 May 1951.** *O. Carter*

The 1.12pm (SO) Stockport Tiviot Dale-Liverpool Central departs from Partington station and begins its climb to cross the Manchester Ship Canal over Cadishead Viaduct on 12 September 1964. *N. F. W. Dyckhoff*

A small boy waves but the fishermen are undisturbed as the DMU, Derby Works Driving Trailer Composite M56233 leading, forming the 3.32pm Stockport Tiviot Dale-Warrington Central crosses the Bridgewater Canal between Skelton Jn and West Timperley on 12 September 1964. MSJ&AR catenaries are visible in the distance. *N. F. W. Dyckhoff*

40

*Top left:*
**Skelton Jn was the hub of the CLC system round South Manchester. This view looking west shows the LNWR line to Broadheath curving left, the CLC line to Glazebrook straight ahead and the connection with the MSJ&AR curving right. In the centre lie sidings and turntable.**
*Collection of J. M. Ryan*

*Bottom left:*
**A present day view 21 July 1983 also taken from the signalbox, shows how the lines have changed. That on the left is still in use. The centre tracks to Glazebrook have been singled further on and this route is now closed. While the line to the right is still busy, the whole central complex of trackwork has been lifted.** *N. F. W. Dyckhoff*

*Above:*
**The 'Hadrian Pullman' hauled by ex-LMS 'Princess Coronation' class 4-6-2 No 46229** *Duchess of Hamilton* **eases past Skelton Junction signalbox on 18 July 1981.**
*W. A. Corkhill*

*Below:*
**Ex-LMS Hughes/Fowler 2-6-0 No 42709 steams away from Skelton Junction towards Baguley with a Blackpool-Nottingham summer Saturday train, September 1957.**
*J. Davenport*

*Top left:*
**WD 2-8-0 No 90010 attacks the 1 in 75 climb to Baguley station with the 6.05am (MO) empty wagon train from Dee Marsh Junction to Godley Junction on 27 January 1964.** *N. F. W. Dyckhoff*

*Bottom left:*
**The crossing keeper's cottage has been modernised and vegetation now grows closer to the track in the absence of steam, but otherwise the scene is the same on 21 July 1983. In latest British Rail livery, Class 56 No 56.093 heads its train of empty MGRs from Fiddlers Ferry en route to Yorkshire.** *N. F. W. Dyckhoff*

*Above:*
**Put up in 1870 to replace the level crossing, this cast iron bridge was colourfully repainted in 1982. Vandals have attacked the road side but not yet the railway side. The other photographs on these pages were taken from this bridge which has itself been taken from the cab of a Class 25 locomotive hauling an ICI limestone train on 20 July 1983.** *N. F. W. Dyckhoff*

*Below:*
**Baguley station sleeps gently in the sun c1935. The island platform was used by an Altrincham-Stockport service withdrawn in 1931 and known to locals as the 'Baguley Bus'.** *Locomotive & General 9795*

*Left:*
A broadside view of Baguley station c1963 showing (left to right) station buildings, cottages, platform shed, footbridge and signalbox.  *N. F. W. Dyckhoff*

*Centre left:*
Baguley station frontage in the days when Timperley was Manchester's market garden rather than just another suburb.  *Collection of J. M. Ryan*

*Bottom left:*
The signalman poses proudly at the door of Baguley box. Perhaps he is also the gardener and responsible for the magnificent display on the platform.
*Collection of J. M. Ryan*

*Below:*
LNER Class 01 2-8-0 No 3578 on a power station coal train between Baguley and Northenden, 9 March 1948.
*J. F. Russell-Smith NRM (Crown Copyright)*

*Above:*
**On their way to the scrap yard. Four steam locomotives are hauled towards Northenden by a well turned out Type 4 English Electric diesel locomotive No D354 in 1964.**
*N. F. W. Dyckhoff*

*Below:*
**Not often seen on this section of the CLC, LNER Class D10 No 2653** *Sir Edward Fraser* **with the 3.23pm Stockport Tiviot Dale-Warrington Central train between Northenden and Baguley on 26 June 1948.** *J. D. Darby*

*Right:*
**With cattle truck in tow, one of the four CLC Sentinel rail cars, No 601, scuttles towards Northenden.** *L Hobdey*

*Top:*
**An ex-LNWR Class 7F 0-8-0 pulls a mixed freight towards Northenden on 25 February 1948.**
*J. F. Russell-Smith NRM (Crown Copyright)*

*Above:*
**Midland Railway 4-4-0 No 443 heads a through train c1920 on the down line and past a fine pair of lattice lower quadrant distant signals showing the CLC practice of putting arms on both sides of the post. Now forgotten, fields of corn stooks fill the background.** *L. Hobdey*

*Right:*
**A closer view of the pair of distant signals. Top left is the Baguley distant. Facing the up line are the splitting distants for Northenden Jn. Right for Stockport Edgeley, left for Cheadle Jn. The train is the 10.15am Warrington-Stockport on 20 July 1963 hauled by Stanier 2-6-4T No 42491.** *Mailpost. N. F. W. Dyckhoff*

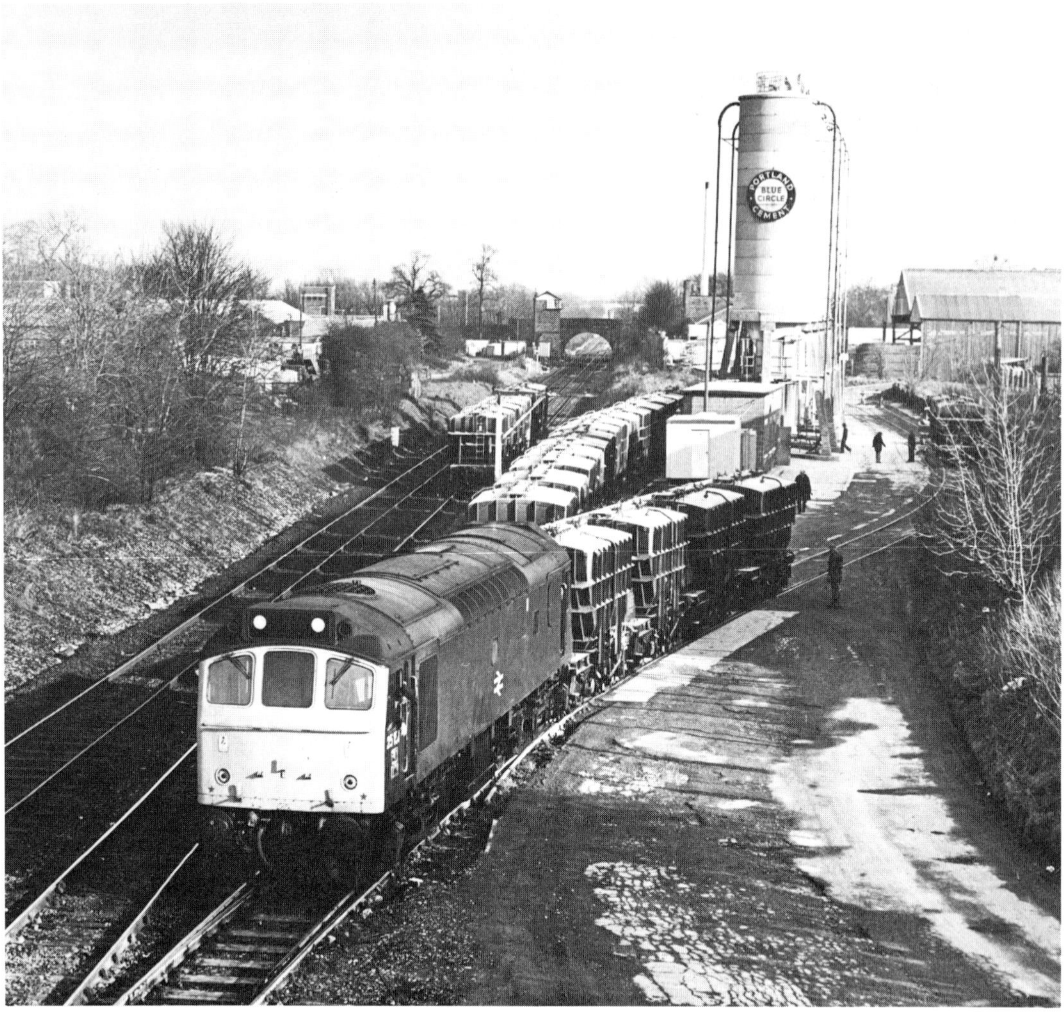
PORTLAND
BLUE CIRCLE
CEMENT

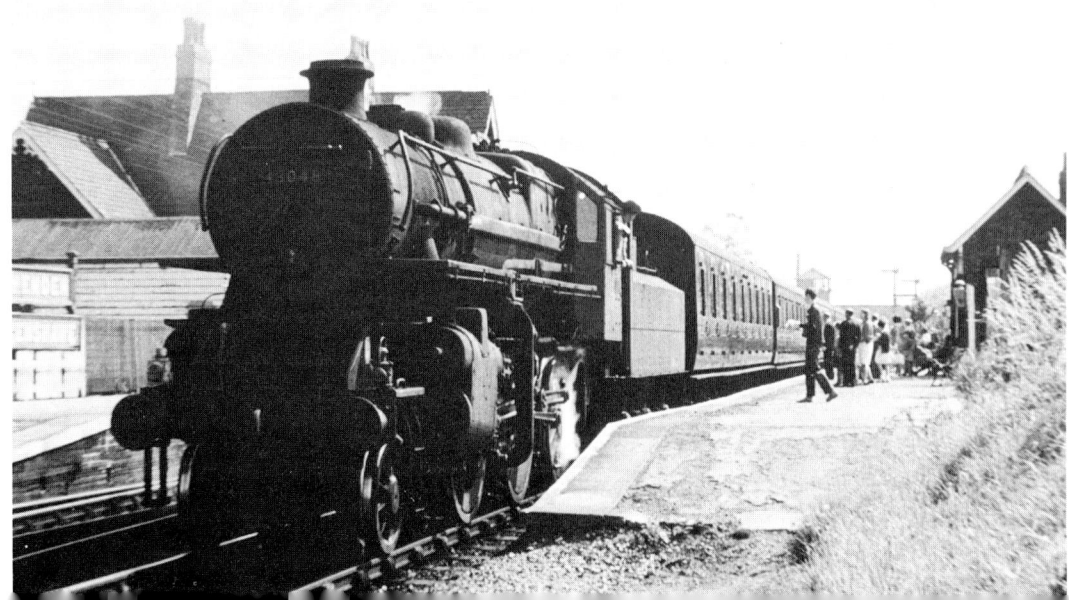

*Top left:*
**The goods yard at Northenden station remains in use as a cement distribution terminal. No 25.154 delivers its loaded wagons ex-Earles Sidings. 'Rose Hill', the old home of Sir Edward Watkin lies behind the trees in the left background.** *Steve Turner*

*Bottom left:*
**Ex-LMS Ivatt Class 4MT 2-6-0 No 43048 comes to a halt at Northenden station down platform with a summer excursion train on 27 July 1963.**
*Mailpost. N. F. W. Dyckhoff*

*Above:*
**The 10.37am (SO) Sheffield Midland-Llandudno train races through Northenden station hauled by ex-LNER Class B1 No 61093 on 4 July 1964.** *N. F. W. Dyckhoff*

*Right:*
**A Warrington-Stockport local train starts away towards Northenden Jn behind LNER Class D9 4-4-0 No 2309 c1949.** *N. F. W. Dyckhoff*

During the electrification of the line between Manchester, London Road and Crewe in 1956, many expresses were diverted over the CLC via Stockport Edgeley, Northenden Jn, Skelton Jn, Northwich and Middlewich. One of these trains headed by ex-LMS 'Patriot' Class 4-6-0 No 45520 *Llandudno* passes Northenden Junction signalbox.
*J. Hill-Wilson*

*Above:*
**Steam hides the signalbox as BR Standard Class 4MT 4-6-0 No 75064 runs its empty wagon train across the junction and heads for Godley on 18 October 1964.**
*N. F. W. Dyckhoff*

*Below:*
**A view from the bridge as immaculate 'Britannia' class 4-6-2 No 70017 *Arrow* brings its train off the ex-LMS line. Most unusually for this date (23 May 1963) a loaded BR Standard cattle wagon is coupled behind the locomotive.**
*N. F. W. Dyckhoff*

**How the sylvan scene has changed.**

*Below:*
**An unidentified Stanier 2-8-0 from Heaton Mersey shed accelerates its train through Northenden Jn in the spring of the last year of steam — 1968.** *N. F. W. Dyckhoff*

*Right:*
**Fifteen years later, on 29 March 1983, new roads cross the landscape and Northenden refuse transfer station fills the right foreground. Class 47 No 47.317 runs round its container trucks.** *Steve Turner*

*Above:*
**Between Northenden Jn and Cheadle Jn, the CLC traverses attractive country, now scarred by the M63 to Stockport. Ex-LMS Fowler Class 7F 0-8-0 No 49547 hauls a down freight c1951.** *N. F. W. Dyckhoff*

*Below:*
**Before Kingsway was extended parallel to the ex-LNWR Styal line which crosses in the distance and long before motorways, LNER 'D6' 4-4-0 No 5855 heads a Liverpool Central-Stockport Tiviot Dale train towards Cheadle station in July 1940.** *W. Potter*

So grimy as to be anonymous, a BR Standard 2-10-0 coasts its empty wagon train under the electrified Styal line and towards Cheadle in May 1968. *N. F. W. Dyckhoff*

*Above:*
Like so many rural stations, Cheadle CLC lay a considerable distance from the village and traffic suffered as a result. Built in the same style as Baguley and Northenden, unlike them it has not been demolished. Plans are in hand to convert it into a pub with brewery and garden centre adjoining. Here an LMS Class 4F 0-6-0 No 4261 passes with a goods train in June 1939. *W. Potter*

*Centre right:*
In the 1930s some weekday local services between Liverpool and Stockport were worked by one of the CLC's four Sentinel rail cars. No 601 stops at Cheadle station up platform in May 1938. It is painted in the earlier two colour livery described by an eye witness as dark tan and light tan boot polish. Later they were painted all over dark brown. *W. Potter*

*Bottom right:*
LNER Class B9 4-6-0 No 6015 works hard on a Stockport-Liverpool train near Cheadle station in August 1945. *W. Potter*

Cheadle West signalbox is in dire need of repair. Stanier 2-6-2T No 40203 from Brunswick shed heads a Stockport-Liverpool train on 1 September 1952. The transfer sidings on the right were laid down by the Midland Railway at the time the Cheadle Heath line was built. A sewage works now occupies the site. *N. E. Preedy*

Painters are busy on the bridge carrying the CLC over the River Mersey as Class J10 0-6-0 No 65209 crosses with a down goods on 3 November 1952. In the background is the bridge carrying the Midland line from Manchester Central to Cheadle Heath. *N. E. Preedy*

*Above:*
**Heaton Mersey had a large locomotive shed (hidden behind the signalbox) and extensive sidings. Ex-LNER Class K3 2-6-0 No 61862 leaves Stockport behind and passes Heaton Mersey signalbox on 30 July 1952.**
*N. E. Preedy*

*Below:*
**The last passenger train working and steam special to run through Stockport from east to west before a landslip closed the line. Rebuilt ex-SR 'Merchant Navy' class 4-6-2 No 35028** *Clan Line* **heads the train at Georges Road Jn on 21 June 1980. In the background is the viaduct carrying the electrified line from Manchester Piccadilly to Crewe via Stockport Edgeley and to which many former CLC freight services have now been diverted.** *Keith Allen*

*Above:*
The distinctive frontage and cobbled forecourt at
Stockport Teviot Dale in August 1964. (This was the
original spelling of the name, later changed.) *John Clarke*

*Below:*
The last passenger train on the Stockport Tiviot Dale to
Liverpool Central service waits to leave at 5.20pm headed
by Stanier 'Black Five' No 44732 on 28 November 1964.
Overhead is the unusual curved and covered footbridge.
*John Clarke*

*Above:*
**Stockport Tiviot Dale was also used by Midland Railway and later LMS, trains between Manchester Central and the South. Compound 4-4-0 No 40927 makes a clean start with the 2.50pm train from Manchester Central-Derby on 1 June 1957.** *N. E. Preedy*

*Right:*
**These were not the only class of compounds to visit Tiviot Dale as is evidenced by this view of GCR Class 8D 4-4-2 No 259, one of four Robinson-designed Compound Atlantics, with the royal train on 7 July 1908. It had brought the Prince of Wales from Northgate station at Chester to open the new Stockport Town Hall.**
*Collection of T. Tattershall*

*Below:*
**General view of Tiviot Dale station east end on 16 March 1948. LNER Class D9 No 2305 is by the signalbox.**
*N. Fields*

*Left:*
**Compound No 40927 continues away
from Stockport Tiviot Dale station and
passes LNER Class 04/7 No 63603 at
the head of a down freight on 1 June
1957.** *T. Lewis*

*Below:*
**On a cold winter afternoon in February
1965 Stanier 2-6-0 No 42975 pounds
up the gradient from Portwood, east of
Stockport and approaches Bredbury Jn
with a freight for Dewsnap sidings.**
*J. R. Hillier*

*Right:*
**Hughes/Fowler 2-6-0 No 42859 runs away from Bredbury Jn with an up empty mineral train on 9 October 1965. The viaduct carries the line from Manchester London Road (now Piccadilly) to Romiley and Marple.** *N. Fields*

*Below:*
**Stanier 2-8-0 No 48252 climbs the steepest main line gradient on the CLC, 1 in 61 past Bredbury, with its train of empty mineral wagons on 10 April 1968.** *J. H. Cooper-Smith*

*Left:*
Banked at the rear Stanier 2-8-0 No 48252 breasts the bank at Woodley Jn on 28 December 1967. The ground frame on the right, with its unusual open cabin, controlled the sidings. *Ian R. Smith*

*Above:*
Another train of empty mineral wagons for Godley Jn hauled by 2-8-0 No 48322 curves on to the short stretch of non-CLC line between Woodley Jn and Apethorne Jn on 6 April 1968. *Brian Stephenson*

*Right:*
Brookfold signalbox guarded the CLC side of Godley Jn where its trains joined the 1,500V DC electrified LNER route over Woodhead. The line to Sheffield is closed with services terminating at Hadfield after reversal at Glossop, and CLC trains no longer come from Cheadle Junction. Only the demolition men are awaited on 13 October 1983. *N. F. W. Dyckhoff*

91

# The North Liverpool Lines and Southport Extension Railway

CATEACRE STATION

*Above:*
**Gateacre and Woolton station from the road showing the covered way between station building and platform. The only other example of a covered way of this type was at Irlam for Cadishead station.** *Collection of J. M. Ryan*

*Below:*
**Platform view of Gateacre station, of lightweight construction because built on an embankment. The covered awning can be seen on the right and the CLC style of painting is well displayed.** *Collection of J. M. Ryan*

*Top right:*
**A Stanier 2-6-2T passes the signalbox and enters West**

Derby station with a Liverpool Central-Southport Lord Street local train in 1951. *J. B. Horne*

*Centre right:*
**West Derby station with the main buildings on the road bridge and the goods yard visible through the arch of the bridge.** *Collection of J. M. Ryan*

*Bottom right:*
**Grand National Day, 30 March 1963, at Aintree Central station. Ex-LMS 'Jubilee' Class 4-6-0 No 45653** *Barham* **heads a train for King's Norton, Class 5 4-6-0 No 44964 one for Manchester Central. A pair of CLC cottages are on the skyline.** *F. Dean*

*Top left:*
Clean in LNER apple green livery but still with a GCR cast numberplate on its cabside, Class X4 4-2-2 No 968 stands at Walton-on-the-Hill shed on 25 April 1925. *W. Potter*

*Centre left:*
Ex-L&YR Class 0F 0-4-0ST No 11231 and ex-GCR LNER Class N5 0-6-2T No 5941 wait by the coaling stage at Walton-on-the-Hill in July 1934. *F. Dean*

*Bottom left:*
Midland and later LMS engines, working through to the Liverpool area were shedded at Walton-on-the-Hill. Still in

MR livery Class 2F 0-6-0 No 3167 stands beside ex-GCR LNER Class J10 0-6-0 No 5196 in August 1927. *F. Dean*

*Above:*
Huskisson goods warehouse was blitzed and destroyed in World War 2. The CLC had plans to rebuild it but this was eventually done by British Railways. Photo taken 18 July 1960. *Collection of R. W. Miller*

*Below:*
Class N5 No 69265, only a few months away from withdrawal, shunts at Huskisson on 3 August 1957. *J. A. Peden*

*Top left:*
A special train of enthusiasts makes a last visit to the Southport Extension Railway on 6 June 1959 and stops at Altcar and Hillhouse station. Sefton and Maghull was built to the same design, also in brick. Both closed 7 January 1952 with the through goods services via Hillhouse Jn stopping two weeks later. For many years the L&YR and later LMS ran a local service from Altcar station to **Southport Chapel Street,** branching from the CLC at **Hillhouse Jn.** Locally it was known as 'Altcar Bob'.
*H. C. Casserley*

*Centre left:*
A Southport train enters Altcar and Hillhouse station hauled by an ex-LMS Compound. *N. Fields*

*Bottom left:*
Woodvale station originally called Woodville and Ainsdale was beautifully kept for many years and had the station name formed in box hedge on the platform. A similar feature was at Northenden station in the early 1900s.
*Collection of J. M. Ryan*

*Top:*
**Ainsdale Beach station signalbox and crossing.**
*Locomotive & General R6971*

*Above:*
A general view of Seaside station (later called Ainsdale Beach) and hotel. Today the latter remains as do the cottages but Coastal Road runs over the railway from Birkdale Palace to Woodvale and a roundabout has taken the place of the level crossing. *Collection of J. M. Ryan*

*Below:*
Birkdale Palace station with a special train formed of 13 GCR six-wheel coaches; the two nearest the camera are saloons. The station master's house is in the background, similar ones were built at Halewood, West Timperley and Godley Jn. *Collection of J. M. Ryan*

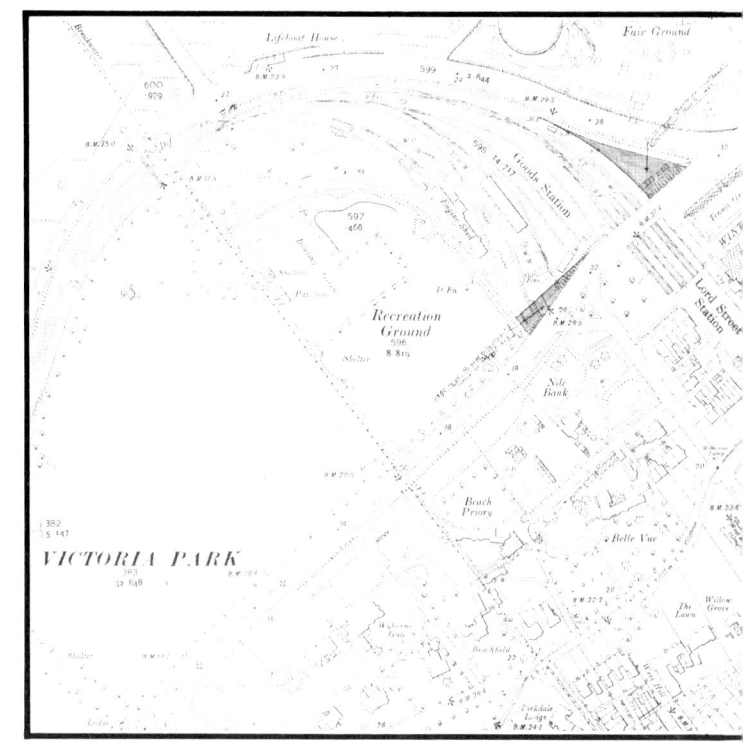

*Above:*
**A general view of Southport Lord Street station on 2 June 1951. Ex-LNER Class D16 4-4-0 No 62536 leaves with one special train while Thompson Class B1 4-6-0 No 61162 and Class J11 No 64420 wait to depart with others.** *N. Fields*

*Below:*
**With the funfair in the background, GCR Class 11A No 878 (originally designed by Pollitt for use on the London Extension) leaves Southport with a train of empty CLC stock c1922.** *Locomotive & General 20011*

*Above:*
Interior of Lord Street station on 2 June 1951 with
Compound 4-4-0 No 41195 standing at the buffer stops.
Today this view is unchanged except that the platforms
have been filled in and buses stand between the pillars.
*N. Fields*

*Below:*
Southport shed with ex-GER 'D16' No 62536 and 'B1'
No 61162 on 2 June 1951.  *N. Fields*

*Right:*
Although now a bus station, the exterior of Southport Lord
Street station is relatively unaltered as this 22 July 1983
view shows. The date, 1884 and the initials, S&CLER
have been covered up below the clock.  *N. F. W. Dyckhoff*

# The Branches

*Above:*
**Shore Road goods station one of the two depots established by the CLC in Birkenhead on the opposite bank of the Mersey was not physically connected with their system. Opened on 1 July 1871 it was reached via Helsby (West Cheshire Junction) and the Birkenhead Joint Line. CLC engines were stabled on the site, the engine shed is just visible between the nameboard and the footbridge on the photograph.**
*NRM (Crown Copyright)*

*Left:*
**A number of small branches served the saltworks near Northwich. Ex LMS Class 2MT 2-6-0 No 46517 stands at the end of the Marston Salt Branch with a LCGB Brake Van Tour on 20 August 1966.** *B. Walker*

*Top right:*
Helsby and Alvanley station was built by the West Cheshire Railway on its line from Northwich to Helsby Jn which opened on 1 September 1869 for goods and 22 June 1870 for passengers. The station staff pose with an MS&LR Sacré 0-6-0 c1905. The view is looking towards Helsby Jn.
*Collection of W. Egerton*

*Centre right:*
This design of postcard was produced by the Cynicus publishing company of Tayport, Fife and printed with the names of different lines, sold widely. Originally posted from Winsford, this card applies to the Winsford branch which was $6\frac{1}{2}$ miles of single track and ran from Winsford Jn near Cuddington on the Manchester-Chester main line. Watkin had intended to extend this branch to meet the North Staffordshire Railway but his partners would not support him and the attempt failed.
*Collection of J. M. Ryan*

*Below:*
Over the years the branch to Winsford and Over station was the subject of much argument; opened in 1870 passenger services were discontinued between 1874 and 1886 following an accident and again from 1888 to 1891. Reinstated in 1892, final withdrawal was proposed for 1931 due to heavy losses, but was only achieved after a hearing before the Railway and Canal Commission. An RCTS special hauled by Class C13 No 67436 and pulling a pair of clerestorey coaches stands in the station shortly before final closure to goods traffic on 17 October 1953.
*N. Fields*

WINSFORD TO CUDDINGTON EXPRESS
via FALK'S JUNCTION AND WHITEGATE

*Below:*
CLC signals were substantially built to a style of their own. This twin-posted bracket with upper quadrant BR arms guards Throstle Nest Jn — the takeoff point for the branch to Chorlton Jn. Photo taken 17 April 1964.  *H. A. Gamble*

*Below right:*
A number of short tunnels were necessary as the South District line approached Throstle Nest Jn. Throstle Nest tunnel No 3 split to form 3 and 3A when the triangle was installed at the turn of the century and Talbot Road crosses tunnel 3A. The MSJ&AR bridge is in the distance; 22 July 1983.  *N. F. W. Dyckhoff*

*Bottom:*
Chorlton-cum-Hardy station was, like the stations at Withington, Didsbury, and Heaton Mersey built in MS&LR style. This is because when they were being planned the MSDR was part of the Sheffield and Midland Committee. Later transferred to the Midland Railway, the section between Throstle Nest Jn and Chorlton-cum-Hardy Jn finally became part of the CLC. Midland awnings shelter the platforms as a Manchester Central-Sheffield train passes through headed by Stanier Class 5 4-6-0 No 44815 in 1951.  *N. F. W. Dyckhoff*

In the same way that Gorton used the line from
Manchester Central to Chester for running in new and
overhauled locomotives, so did Derby use its line to
Manchester Central. This took many interesting
locomotives along the short stretch of CLC from Chorlton
Jn. Here the Beyer-Ljungstrom 4-6-6-4 condensing turbine
locomotive halts at Chorlton-cum-Hardy station in 1926.
Later years saw the diesels 10000 and 10001 as well as the
Fell 4-8-4 which also ran trials on the CLC main line to
Liverpool Central in March 1954.
*Collection of R. W. Miller*

*Below:*
Only a single line curving round to Fairfield remains today
at Chorlton Jn. The straight line to Heaton Mersey has
been lifted.   *N. F. W. Dyckhoff*

# Miscellanea

*Top left:*
**Staff at West Timperley Street.**
*Manchester Polytechnic Manchester Studies Unit*

*Bottom left:*
**Great Central railwaymen pose with their CLC colleagues in front of a Class N5 0-6-2T at Warrington Central.**
*Warrington Museum & Art Gallery*

*Above:*
**One for the family album; a porter from Warrington station.** *Warrington Museum & Art Gallery*

*Above right:*
**James Pinion, Manager Cheshire Lines Railway 1904-1910. The photograph is taken from the souvenir album of photographs presented to him by 'His brother officers on the occasion of his retirement' in July 1910.**
*County Down Museum Preservation Trust*

*Right:*
**An engine crew at Northwich shed on their Class 25 locomotive in 1967.** *Collection of W. Egerton*

*Left:*
Composite No 316 built at Doncaster in 1911 for the Manchester-Liverpool Service. The photograph shows the interior of a first class compartment.
*NRM (Crown Copyright)*

*Below:*
First Class family saloon No 201 built at Doncaster works in 1912. It replaced 6-wheel saloon No 201 built for the CLC by the MS&LR in 1877. In the 1907 Appendix to the working timetable the allocation of Cheshire Lines saloon carriages is given as five at Liverpool (two first class including 201, and three third class); six third class at Manchester; one third class at Southport and one third class at Chester. No 201 lasted long enough to be nationalised and to wear the British Railways crimson lake/cream livery.
*NRM (Crown Copyright)*

*Top right:*
Five ton refrigerated meat van No 300 built at Doncaster in 1909. A pure Great Northern design, the livery is believed to have been white with black letters shaded in red.
*NRM (Crown Copyright)*

*Centre right:*
ICI limestone hopper built, to this design, from 1935 by Charles Roberts for the traffic between Tunstead and Winnington (Northwich). The hoppers run in block trains and after loading, wait a couple of hours before returning to Winnington. During this time they are maintained as necessary. Piles of brake blocks are in the foreground of this 20 July 1983 picture.
*N. F. W. Dyckhoff*

*Bottom right:*
CLC sheeted wagons at ICI Lostock works c1915. The zig-zag edged style of white lines was in use from the very early days of the CLC.
*ICI Mond Division*

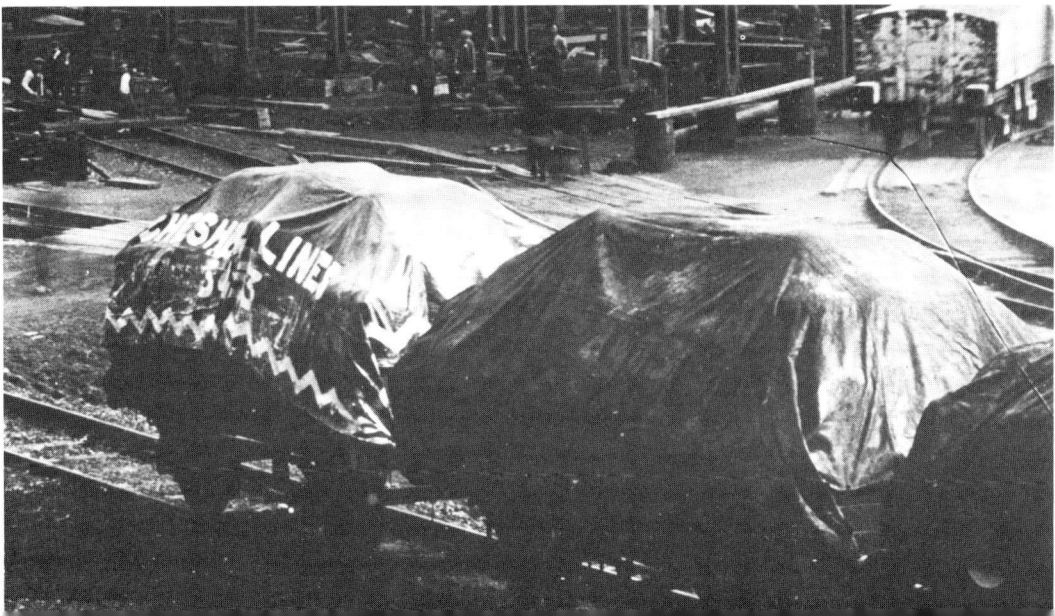

| | 370 | 371 | 372 | 373 | 374 | 375 | 376 | 377 | 378 | 379 | 380 | 381 | 382 | 383 | 384 | 385 | 386 | 387 | 388 | 389 | 390 |
|---|---|---|---|---|---|---|---|---|---|---|---|---|---|---|---|---|---|---|---|---|---|
| **DOWN TRAINS.** **WEEK DAYS.** | 10.55 a.m. Express Goods Copley Hill to Garston | 1.50 p.m. L.N.E. Through Goods ex Mottram Yard | L.N.E. EXPRESS PASSENGER to Harwich | 2.26 p.m. L.N.E. Mineral ex Mottram Yard | L.N.E. Through Goods to Bidston | Through Goods | L.N.E. EXPRESS PASSENGER to Cleethorpes | L.N.E. Cattle for Sheffield | L.M.S. PASSENGER to Derby | L.N.E. Through Goods to Dewsnap | EXPRESS PASSENGER | 3.5 p.m. PASSENGER ex Southport | 3.0 p.m. Through Goods Huskisson to Gidlton due 5 to p.m | SEASON L.M.S. 1.25 p.m Leeds to Llandudno | PASSENGER Steam Coach (SX) Steam Train (SO) | Engine and Brake | Empty Steam Coach | Through Goods | L.N.E. PASSENGER to St. Helens | 2 p.m PASSENGER ex Hayfield | 3.3 p.m. L.N.E. Express Goods ex Mottram Yard |
| Class........ | | | B | | C | B | B | | 2 | | C | | | B | | | | B | | | 2 |
| | SX Q | MO | | | SO | SO | MSX | MFSO | TO | | | HC | SO A | SO K | | | SO | | SX J | SX | MX |
| | p.m. | p.m. | p.m. | P.M. | p.m | p.m | p.m. | p.m. | p.m. | p.m. | p.m. | p.m. | p.m. | p.m. | p.m. | p.m. | p.m. | p.m. | p.m. | p.m. | p.m. |
| CODLEY JUNCTION ... dep. | | 2 10 | ... | 2 26 | 2 35 | 2 35 | | ... | ... | ... | ... | ... | ... | 3 10 | ... | ... | ... | ... | ... | ... | 3 15 |
| Woodley Junction...... ,, | | 2 20 | ... | 2 36 | 2 45 | 2 45 | | ... | ... | ... | ... | ... | ... | 3 16 | ... | ... | ... | ... | ... | ... | 3 23 |
| Bredbury Junction ... pass | | 2 29 | ... | 2 45 | 2 54 | 2 54 | | ... | ... | ... | ... | ... | ... | 3 20 | ... | ... | ... | ... | 3 23 | 3 27 | |
| Brinnington Junc. ,, | | 2 38 | ... | 2 54 | 3 3 | 3 3 | | ... | ... | ... | ... | ... | ... | 3 22 | ... | ... | ... | ... | 3 25 | 3 31 | |
| Portwood ... dep. | | ... | ... | ... | ... | ... | | ... | ... | ... | ... | ... | ... | ... | ... | ... | ... | ... | ... | ... | |
| STOCKPORT { arr. | | ... | ... | ... | ... | ... | | ... | ... | ... | ... | ... | ... | 3 23 | ... | ... | ... | ... | 3 27 | | |
| (TIVIOT DALE) { dep. | | 2 40 | ... | 2 56 | 3 5 | 3 5 | | ... | ... | ... | ... | ... | ... | 3 24 | ... | ... | 3†28 | ... | ... | 3 33 | |
| HEATON MERSEY { arr. | | ... | ... | ... | ... | 3 10 | | ... | ... | ... | ... | ... | ... | ... | ... | ... | 3†*36 | ... | ... | | |
| SIDINGS { dep. | | 2 45 | ... | ... | 3 13 | 3 10 | | ... | ... | ... | ... | ... | ... | ... | 3 30 | ... | ... | ... | ... | 3 38 | |
| MANCHESTER (C.) ... { arr. | | ... | ... | ... | ... | ... | | ... | ... | ... | ... | ... | ... | ... | ... | ... | ... | ... | ... | | |
| Cheadle Junction ...... dep. | | ... | ... | ... | ... | ... | | ... | ... | ... | ... | ... | ... | ... | ... | ... | ... | ... | ... | | |
| Cheadle West { arr. dep. | | ... | ... | ... | ... | ... | | ... | ... | ... | ... | ... | ... | ... | ... | ... | ... | ... | ... | | |
| Cheadle Station.......... ,, | | ... | ... | ... | ... | ... | SUSPENDED | ... | ... | ... | ... | ... | ... | ... | M | ... | ... | ... | ... | | |
| Northenden ,, | 2 44 | 2 52 | ... | ... | 3 8 | 3 18 | | ... | ... | ... | ... | ... | 3 30 | 3 32 | 3 39 | ... | ... | ... | ... | 3 44 | |
| Baguley ,, | | ... | ... | ... | ... | ... | | ... | ... | ... | ... | ... | ... | 3 37 | ... | ... | ... | ... | ... | | |
| SKELTON JUNCTION { arr. dep. | 2 52 | 3 0 | ... | ... | 3 16 | 3 25 | | ... | ... | ... | ... | ... | 3 37 | 3 39 | 3 39 | ... | ... | ... | ... | 3 51 | |
| West Timperley.......... ,, | | ... | ... | ... | ... | ... | | ... | ... | ... | ... | ... | ... | 3 42 | ... | ... | ... | ... | ... | | |
| Partington Station ... ,, | | ... | ... | ... | ... | ... | | ... | ... | ... | ... | ... | ... | 3 47 | ... | ... | ... | ... | ... | | |
| Cadishead ,, | | ... | ... | ... | ... | ... | | ... | ... | ... | ... | ... | ... | 3 50 | ... | ... | ... | ... | ... | | |
| MANCHESTER (C.) dep. | | ... | 3 10 | ... | ... | ... | 3 20 | 3 25 | 3 30 | ... | ... | ... | ... | 3 33 | ... | ... | ... | ... | | |

*(Column 385: "Loco for Coaling". Column 389: "Birch Vale dep. 3 5, New Mills 3 10, Marple 3 16, Romiley 3 20 p.m.")*

**Left:**

A selection of CLC tickets [(i) (ii) and (iii) across]

*Row 1:* Examples of early singles. (ii) has been dated with the small typeface favoured by the Midland Railway.

*Row 2:* Later singles showing (i) Pre-Grouping CLC (ii) LMS and (iii) LNER prints. The CLC printed their own tickets (at Warrington Works) from 1886 until 1933.

*Row 3:* Examples of special singles

(i) Emigrant. Three quarters of all emigrants sailed from Liverpool. This ticket was possibly used by emigrants when their sailing was diverted to Cardiff.

(ii) Trans Britain. A reminder of the shorter trans-Atlantic route used by many European/Scandinavian emigrants.

(iii) Ships crew. Reduced fare ticket issued by the LNER agency in Tower Buildings — but an LMS print.

*Row 4:* (i) Period return — LMS type.

(ii) Special return for the use of the CLC Recreation & Welfare Association. Their ground was next to Allerton engine shed and Garston was the nearest CLC station.

(iii) Ticket for a through journey to the Isle of Man via IoMSPC.

*Row 5:* Examples of tickets covering river and road journeys. (All LMS prints).

*Row 6:* (i) Pre-Grouping dog ticket (actually issued 1933).

(ii) Weekly workman (LMS print).

(iii) Platform ticket (LMS print).

**Above:**

Excerpt from working timetables from 27 September 1937 showing services from Godley Junction. Note the use of a steam coach between Godley Junction and Liverpool Central on weekday trains.

**Right:**

Page from Appendix to the working timetables, 4 November 1935.

---

### UP AND DOWN LINES.

As it is convenient in the issue of Instructions respecting Signal and Working Arrangements to distinguish the different lines of Rails by the terms Up and Down, and in order that no misunderstanding should exist on the subject, the following information is given for the guidance of the Staff:—

| UP LINES. | DOWN LINES. |
|---|---|
| Liverpool to Manchester. | Manchester to Liverpool. |
| Huskisson to Fazakerley South Junction. | Fazakerley South Junction to Huskisson. |
| Fazakerley West Junction to Fazakerley North Junction. | Fazakerley North Junction to Fazakerley West Junction. |
| Southport to Halewood East Junction. | Halewood East Junction to Southport. |
| Hunt's Cross East Junction to Halewood North Junction. | Halewood North Junction to Hunt's Cross East Junction. |
| Dam Lane Junction to Moss Box. | Moss Box to Dam Lane Junction. |
| Glazebrook East Junction to Woodley Junction. | Woodley Junction to Glazebrook East Junction. |
| Trafford Park Junction to Throstle Nest South Junction. | Throstle Nest South Junction to Trafford Park Junction. |
| Throstle Nest East Junction to Chorlton Junc. | Chorlton Junction to Throstle Nest East Junc. |
| Apethorne Junction to Godley Junction. | Godley Junction to Apethorne Junction. |
| Deansgate Junction to Skelton Junction. | Skelton Junction to Deansgate Junction. |
| Old Trafford Junction to Cornbrook West Junc. | Cornbrook West Junction to Old Trafford Junc. |
| Chester to Altrincham. | Altrincham to Chester. |

### ENGINE TURNTABLES.

| Place. | Length of rail on turntable. | Place. | Length of rail on turntable. |
|---|---|---|---|
| Liverpool Central | 50 ft. | Heaton Mersey Loco... | 50 ft. |
| Brunswick Loco. | 60 ft. | Huskisson | 45 ft. |
| Allerton | 50 ft. | Glazebrook Station ... | 45 ft. |
| Southport Loco. | 56 ft. | Godley | 70 ft. |
| Walton Loco. | 50 ft. | Northwich Loco. | 70 ft. |
| Whitecross Sdg., Warrington | 50 ft. | Chester Loco. | 60 ft. |
| Cornbrook | 50 ft. | Helsby Station | 50 ft. |
| Manchester Central | 65 ft. | Skelton Junction | 60 ft. |
| Trafford Park Loco. | { 50 ft. 60 ft. | | |

### LIST OF PLACES WHERE LOCOMOTIVE WATER COLUMNS ARE AVAILABLE.

| | |
|---|---|
| Liverpool Central. | Heaton Mersey Sidings. |
| Brunswick Goods Yard. | Heaton Mersey West Junction. |
| Brunswick Loco. | Heaton Mersey East Junction. |
| Allerton Sidings. | Heaton Mersey Loco. |
| Halewood Sidings. | Stockport Station, |
| Knotty Ash, Up and Down Platforms. | Up and Down Platforms. |
| Walton Loco. | Godley, Up and Down Platforms. |
| Huskisson. | Godley Sidings. |
| Southport, Station and Loco. | Knutsford, Up and Down Platforms. |
| Warrington, Up and Down Platforms. | Northwich, Up and Down Platforms. |
| Warrington Sidings. | Northwich East Sidings. |
| Warrington, Whitecross Sidings. | Northwich Loco. |
| Glazebrook Sidings. | Hartford Sidings. |
| Trafford Park Loco. | Winsford. |
| Trafford Park Sidings. | Delamere, Up and Down Platforms. |
| Cornbrook Sidings. | Helsby Station. |
| Manchester Central. | Chester Loco. |

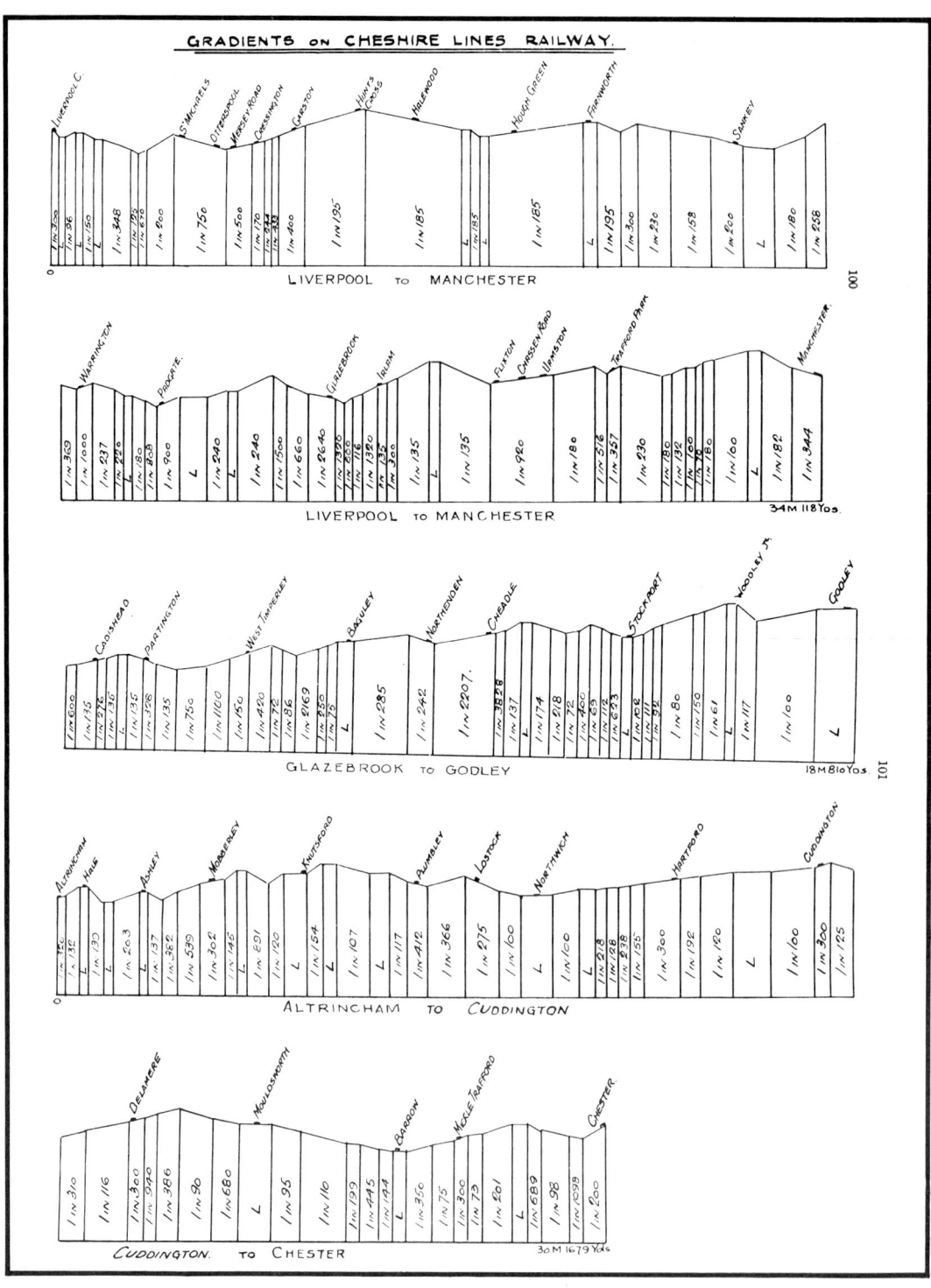

GRADIENTS on CHESHIRE LINES RAILWAY.

LIVERPOOL TO MANCHESTER

LIVERPOOL TO MANCHESTER

GLAZEBROOK TO GODLEY

ALTRINCHAM TO CUDDINGTON

CUDDINGTON TO CHESTER

*Above:*

A selection of gradient profiles taken from the CLC Appendix to the working timetables. Those shown cover the lines still in use today.

*Top right:*

From Cheshire Lines Committee Financial Accounts and Statistical Returns for the year ended 31 December 1921.

| | RUNNING LINES. | | | | | | Sidings reduced to Single Track. | Total of Single Track, including Sidings. | Year 1920. Total of Single Track, including Sidings. |
| --- | --- | --- | --- | --- | --- | --- | --- | --- | --- |
| | Length of Road First Track. | Second Track. | Third Track. | Fourth Track. | Over Four Tracks, (reduced to Single Track). | Total Miles (reduced to Single Track). | | | |
| | M. Ch. | M. Ch. | M. Ch. | M. Ch. | M. Ch. | M. Ch. | M. Ch. | M. Ch. | M. Ch. |
| LINES OWNED BY THE COMMITTEE:— | | | | | | | | | |
| MAIN AND PRINCIPAL LINES:— | | | | | | | | | |
| Liverpool to Manchester including Warrington Straight Line | 37 4 | 37 0 | 6 66 | 4 41 | 1 30 | 86 61 | 61 11 | 147 72 | 147 72 |
| Manchester South District Railway | 2 51 | 2 51 | — | — | — | 5 22 | 0 61 | 6 3 | 6 3 |
| Glazebrook East Junction to Godley including Broadheath, Skelton, Brinnington and Apethorne Junctions | 19 6 | 19 6 | 2 37 | 1 19 | 0 26 | 42 14 | 24 60 | 66 74 | 66 74 |
| Altrincham to Chester including Winsford and Helsby Junctions | 35 3 | 30 79 | — | — | — | 66 2 | 24 48 | 90 50 | 90 48 |
| Hunt's Cross East Junction to Aintree | 14 40 | 14 40 | 1 27 | 1 27 | — | 31 54 | 21 44 | 53 18 | 53 4 |
| TOTAL.—Main and Principal Lines ... | 108 24 | 104 16 | 10 50 | 7 7 | 1 56 | 231 73 | 132 64 | 364 57 | 364 11 |
| MINOR AND BRANCH LINES:— | | | | | | | | | |
| Liverpool to Manchester and Godley, including Wavertree, Huskisson, Birkenhead, Seacombe, Allerton Branch, Glazebrook Curve and Cornbrook Loop | 6 66 | 4 74 | — | — | — | 11 60 | 6 68 | 18 48 | 18 48 |
| Altrincham to Chester, including Northwich Salt, Winnington and Winsford Branches | 14 4 | 1 17 | — | — | — | 15 21 | 4 39 | 19 60 | 19 60 |
| TOTAL | 129 14 | 110 27 | 10 50 | 7 7 | 1 56 | 258 74 | 144 11 | 403 5 | 402 69 |
| LINES LEASED BY THE COMMITTEE:— | | | | | | | | | |
| Southport and Cheshire Lines Extension Rly. | 14 3 | 14 3 | 0 16 | 0 16 | 0 9 | 28 47 | 4 33 | 33 0 | 33 0 |
| TOTAL OF MILES LEASED | 14 3 | 14 3 | 0 16 | 0 16 | 0 9 | 28 47 | 4 33 | 33 0 | 33 0 |
| GRAND TOTAL | 143 17 | 124 30 | 10 66 | 7 23 | 1 65 | 287 41 | 148 44 | 436 5 | 435 69 |

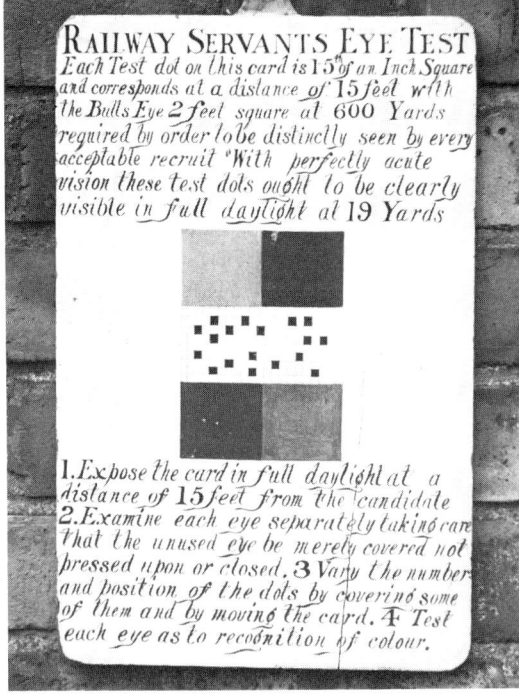

*Right:*
**Handbill for Tarporley Hunt Steeple Chase to which the CLC ran special trains.**

*Above:*
**An eyesight test board from Trafford Park locomotive shed.**

## CHESHIRE LINES.
# TARPORLEY HUNT STEEPLECHASES,
### Wednesday, April 7, 1886.

## Special Trains at Cheap Fares
WILL RUN TO
# CUDDINGTON,
AS UNDER:—

| Stations. | Passengers and Horses. a.m. | 1st and 3rd Class. a.m. | 1st CLASS EXPRESS. a.m. | Fares to CUDDINGTON and Back same Day. 1st Class. | 3rd Class. |
| --- | --- | --- | --- | --- | --- |
| MANCHESTER (Central) ... dep. | 9 10 | 9 35 | 9 55 | | |
| Old Trafford ... ... ... ... | 9 15 | | | | |
| Stretford ... ... ... ... | 9 20 | | 1st Class Only. | 5/- | 2/6 |
| Sale ... ... ... ... | 9 25 | | | | |
| Altrincham ... ... ... | 9 35 | 9 49 | | | |
| Peel Causeway ... ... ... | 9 40 | 9 53 | 10 10 | | |
| Knutsford ... ... ... | 9 55 | 10 12 | 10 20 | 3/6 | 1/9 |
| Northwich ... ... ... | 10 10 | 10 30 | — | 1/9 | -/9 |
| CUDDINGTON ... ... ... arr. | 10 20 | 10 41 | 10 41 | | |

RETURNING FROM CUDDINGTON AS BELOW:
FIRST CLASS EXPRESS at 6 15 p.m. for KNUTSFORD, PEEL CAUSEWAY, and MANCHESTER.
FIRST and THIRD CLASS for all the above Stations at 6 50 p.m.

It is respectfully requested that Horse Boxes be ordered from the respective Station Masters for the 9 10 a.m. Train from Manchester, and the 6 50 p.m. Return Train from Cuddington, as they cannot be conveyed by the Ordinary Trains.

The Tickets will be available on the day of issue, and by the Trains named only. Tickets, Bill, &c., may be had at the Stations; and also in Manchester from Messrs. SWAN and LEACH, 3, Princess Street; Albert Square; Messrs. COOK and SON, 61 Market Street; Mr. BURN, 512, Rochdale Road; Mr. WRAY, 123, Stretford Road; Mr. WILLIAMS, 104, Mow Lane West; and from Mr. TAYLOR, 1, Insell Street.

General Station, Liverpool,
March, 1886.

**D. MELDRUM, Manager.**

McCorquodale & Co., Limited, Railway and General Printers, Liverpool, Warrington, Chester, and London.

*Above:*

**Standard CLC bridgeplate near Padgate, taken on 19 July 1983.** *N. F. W. Dyckhoff*

*Right:*

**CLC standard milepost. M stood for main line and all mileages were measured from Liverpool Central, the Headquarters of the CLC. Photographed at Skelton Junction on 21 July 1983.** *N. F. W. Dyckhoff*

*Below:*

**As stations closed, so their furniture found alternative uses. Platform seats are particularly popular in the garden.** *N. F. W. Dyckhoff*